The Catholic Revolution

*New Wine, Old Wineskins, and
the Second Vatican Council*

Andrew Greeley

UNIVERSITY OF CALIFORNIA PRESS

Berkeley   Los Angeles   London

282.73
GRE
2004

−M−4/04 25.00

University of California Press
Berkeley and Los Angeles, California

University of California Press, Ltd.
London, England

Library of Congress Cataloging-in-Publication Data

Greeley, Andrew M., 1928–
  The Catholic revolution : new wine, old wineskins, and the Second
Vatican Council / Andrew Greeley.
    p. cm.
  Includes bibliographical references and index.
  ISBN 0–520-23817–6 (alk. paper)
    1. Vatican Council (2nd : 1962–1965)   2. Catholic Church—Doc-
trines.   I. Title.

BX830   1962   .G64 2004
282'.73'09045—dc21

                                2003012768

Manufactured in the United States of America
13   12   11   10   09   08   07   06   05   04
10   9   8   7   6   5   4   3   2   1

The paper used in this publication meets the minimum
 requirements of ANSI/NISO Z39.48–1992 (R 1997)
(*Permanence of Paper*).

The Catholic Revolution

In fond memory of Ellen Sewell

Feeble and decadent societies do not undergo revolutions. . . .
Revolutions are perversely a sign of strength and youth in
society.

Crane Brinton, *The Anatomy of Revolution*

I know of no other such assembly in history that undertook
such a bold reshaping of the institution it represented and did
it with more fairness, serenity, and courage.

John W. O'Malley, "Developments, Reforms, and
Two Great Reformations: Towards a Historical
Assessment of Vatican II"

CONTENTS

Conclusion

191

TABLES

TABLES

Introduction

In this extended essay I intend to reprise and refocus my work on American Catholics.[1] I will try to tie together in a reasonably coherent package some of many bits and pieces of research from various studies in which I have participated since 1961. Three theoretical perspectives have aided in this refocusing—William Sewell Jr.'s work on revolutionary events (1996), Melissa Jo Wilde's study of the Second Vatican Council as collective behavior (2002), and my own theories of the Catholic imagination (Greeley 1995, 2000).

My argument will be that the bishops of the world, in the euphoria generated by their (alas temporary) freedom from the obstructions of the Roman Curia, introduced relatively modest changes to the Church that were too much for the rigid structures of nineteenth-century Catholicism to absorb. They poured new wine into old wineskins and the wineskins burst. The changes the Council mandated persuaded the lower clergy and the laity that "unchangeable" Catholicism could change. When the conciliar euphoria spread to them in the late 1960s, they created their own reform, in which they swept away Catholic "rules" that seemed not to make sense. While this revolution was probably over by 1972, the changes have become permanent because the laity and the lower clergy, loyal to the basic doctrines of the Catholic heritage and to the images and stories of the Catholic imagination, no longer accept the Church's right to control their sexual lives. For weal or woe, they have become Catholics on their own terms. Despite the trauma of the revolution and the continuing chaos, most Catholics remain stubbornly Catholic because of the appeal of the sacramentalism and communalism of the tradition. The gap between the higher and lower orders in the Church remains because the former do not understand that in certain matters they have lost all credibility with the latter. Nonetheless, Catholicism survives. The gap will narrow only when the leadership begins to reshape its style of interacting with the laity and the lower clergy in a way that emphasizes the beauty and charm of the Catholic heritage rather than its own claim to absolute authority.

At the very time the mass of laity and lower clergy were carrying out their revolution, a relatively small activist elite attempted its own. Some teachers and members of parish staffs, some liturgists, some ecumenists, some feminists, and some directors of religious education endeavored to sweep out of Catholicism all that seemed irrelevant "in the wake of the Council" (which meant all that they didn't like) without consulting the laity, who were to be "renewed" to fit the elite's model of what it meant to be Catholic. This group, which ran amok in the postconciliar years, produced what Robert Barron has called "beige Catholicism"—Catholicism without metaphor, charm, or beauty. It was as authoritarian as the leaders who tried to stem the tide of change by reverting to the old strategies of repression. Such varied responses are to be expected in revolutionary eras. Some tried to save the old wineskins, others created their own personal wineskins without regard for the traditions of the heritage, good taste, or the personal and intellectual depth and rights of the laity.

My argument is complex and is based on multiple bodies of data. However, the model I propose does marshal the available data into what I think is a coherent analysis and refutes the current tendency to blame Pope John XXIII and his Council for the apparent destruction of Catholicism. I trust that readers will be patient with my occasional reliance on arcane analytic methods. After all, the Catholic revolution is a complex event for which no simple explanations are possible.[2]

I am grateful to Bill Sewell and Melissa Jo Wilde for their theoretical insights (and I dedicate this book to Bill's late wife Ellen, my long-ago research assistant, who left us too soon); to Michael Hout, my doggedly patient colleague for the past two decades; to Albert Bergesen for the insights about religious imagery; and to Mark Chaves, who seems to have every reference in the world at his fingertips and offered valuable insights every step of the way. I am grateful to my coworkers through the years—Peter Rossi, William McCready, Kathleen McCourt, Joan Fee, and Teresa Sullivan. I also owe a deep debt of gratitude to David Tracy, whose book *The Analogical Imagination* has so deeply influenced all my work in the past twenty years. My thanks are also due to the three cardinals who listened patiently to me through the years— Albert Meyer, Joseph Bernardin, and Francis George.

I must insist here at the very beginning that the sociologist's role is to report the facts of a situation and to fit them into a theoretical construct. Just because he reports that something has happened, it does not follow that he approves or advocates what has happened. Many Catholics tend to blame the sociologist for reporting the facts, on the grounds that he is expressing his opinion or has in fact created the situation described. They would rather have him suppress his findings and report the findings they would like "for the good of the Church." But for the sociologist to do that would be as irresponsible as it would be for Church leaders to dismiss research findings because they do not fit their preconceived ideologies or expectations.

PART I

Old Wineskins

ONE

A Catholic Revolution

This book is about the revolutionary impact of the Second Vatican Council on the Catholic Church in the United States. I note at the outset that I do not like the misuse of the word "revolution" as a metaphor, a shallow media paradigm for change. The so-called sexual revolution was not in fact a revolution but an increase in premarital sex along with a decline in age at first sexual activity, an increase in the divorce rate, and a steady increase in nudity in films. There has not been an increase in the frequency of sexual intercourse nor, it would seem, in the satisfaction from that activity. It is still true that most sexual activity (and the most satisfying) is between permanently committed partners. More nudity has not made for better films. Moreover, disapproval of extramarital sex has not declined. Change? Yes. Dramatic change? Perhaps. A complete overturning of values and practices? Hardly.

Most claims of revolution are an abuse of language, abuse that is inevitable when thought must be reduced to fit a 30-second TV clip or a 750-word press release. Before I began to think about this book I was repelled by the notion that the Vatican Council might not only have been a revolutionary event but might also have, unintentionally, incited a sweeping revolution within Catholicism. I did not want to engage in further abuse of the metaphor.

However, I am now forced by theory and data to conclude that there was indeed a revolution within Catholicism in the United States (and in most other countries) in the years immediately after the Vatican Council, which was itself a revolutionary event. The "effervescence" created by the Council had run its course by the early 1970s, though its effects are still felt thirty years later. Attempts to restore the Catholicism of the preconciliar years are doomed to fail because Catholics, particularly those who have come to maturity in the past four decades, no longer recognize the right of the Church leadership to undo the changes made during those critical years. The long reign of Pope John Paul II can be seen in this model as an attempt not so much to repeal the Council itself as to repeal the revolution that swept the Church in the years immediately afterward. This attempt did not succeed, especially when it was directed at the sexual behavior of Catholics, the primary concern of the Church in the twentieth century. Catholics, rightly or wrongly, have withdrawn sexuality from the area in which they feel they have to listen to their Church. The efforts since the birth control encyclical of 1968 to reverse that trend have failed—and indeed probably have been counterproductive.

Would it have been possible for the Church to have presided over a Council (which I will argue was a revolutionary event) and not produce a revolution? If one agrees with Pope John and the fathers of the Council that the Catholic Church had to change, could the effects of that change have been less revolutionary? Perhaps, if the quality of leadership and the scholarship had been strong enough. In fact, however, I doubt it. The leadership lost control of the postconciliar moments largely because of arrogance and ignorance—and perhaps because of what seemed to the laity to be an obsession with sex. Moreover, there was not enough depth among either the leadership or the intellectual class in the Church to cope with revolutionary change. The leadership thought it knew what was happening and what was necessary to stem the tide. However, even a wise and prudent leadership would have been swept away by the floodwaters of the change the Council had created. The fathers of the Council had agreed with Pope John that change was necessary. They had not realized how long overdue the change was and how destabilizing the effects would be on the structures of the Church in which they had been raised. They were, in the words of my title, unaware how devastating the new wine of the Council would be to the old wineskins of a Church still structured to resist the threats of the Enlightenment and the French Revolution. Indeed, they could have decided to enact much less dramatic changes and the effect would have been the same.

Unlike some commentators, I entertain no nostalgia for the so-called confident Church of the years 1945–1960. Most of those who lament the passing of that Church weren't there at the time. Even if the clock could be turned back, what would reappear would be much less appealing than the selective perceptions of those who would like a nice, orderly, "traditional Church."

Nor am I persuaded, as are some in the Vatican, that a strong effort should be made to restore much of the discipline that existed in the preconciliar Church, to undo the mistakes that have been made since 1965 and to protect the Church from even greater harm. Cardinal Joseph Ratzinger would doubtless like to remodel the Church to fit the rural Bavarian paradigm within which he remembers growing up. Everyone thinks his own neighborhood is special: I lament the Catholicism of St. Angela in Chicago, where I grew up, and of Christ the King, where I served just before the Council. However, his Bavaria and my St. Angela and Christ the King are not there anymore, if indeed they ever were. Moreover, their restoration four decades after the Council is impossible. Is that which replaced the Bavarian and Chicago Catholicisms of the late 1950s better or worse? That is a matter of personal judgment. The cardinal (and many, though not most, of the liberal theologians of the Council) think it is worse. I think that it is better and that it will continue to grow and improve as new structures fall into place.

I believe that, for all the confusion, all the mistakes, all the false prophets, all the stupidity of the last thirty-five years of Catholic history, the new Church is a great improvement on the old Church. There have been serious losses, but some of them are perhaps not as serious as they might have seemed. The mass departures from the priesthood and religious life, for example, may mean only that those who were unhappy in their vocations now have a chance to make new starts. I cannot see such an outcome as bad. Nor can I see as bad the enthusiasm for service that can be found in every Catholic parish in the land where the pastor is reasonably secure and reasonably tolerant. I am not disturbed by a Catholic population that, for all the trauma of the years since 1960, is still largely loyal to its Catholic affiliation and still strongly committed to the Catholic doctrines of Trinity, Incarnation, Eucharist, Sacrament, Church, and Papacy. Finally, I am convinced that it was inevitable that once Catholics entered the ranks of the college-educated middle class, they would be less inclined to accept blind obedience as a criterion for moral decision making.

On balance then, I believe that while there is confusion and turbulence in Catholicism as it enters the third millennium, Catholics continue to be Catholic because they like being Catholic. If there had not been a Council in the mid-1960s, the Church would be in far worse confusion than it is now. The revolution had to come. It would have been much better for the Church if it had come earlier; it would have been much worse if it had not come at all.

My arguments in this extended essay are based on three sources—data, observation, and theory. I will try to distinguish in the chapters that follow among the three sources, though they are so intermingled in my experience that at times it will be difficult to do so.

Since 1961 I have been monitoring with the tools of an empirical sociologist the condition of the Catholic Church in the United States (and since 1985 its condition in many other countries). In 1963 Peter Rossi and I conducted a study of the effect of Catholic schooling on adult Catholics under a grant from the Carnegie Foundation (Greeley and Rossi 1966). The national sample data we collected provided the first serious portrait of American Catholics since a study by the *Catholic Digest* in 1952 (the data cards from which had been lost). The Council was in session in 1963, but it seemed that nothing much had happened yet—except a revolutionary event that went unnoticed. Thus the 1963 study provides a useful portrait of American Catholics at the edge of the Vatican Council—perhaps at the edge of an abyss.

Then, in 1974, with a data collection grant from the National
Institute of Education, the National Opinion Research Center
(NORC) conducted a second study of Catholic schools, which I
directed along with William McCready and Kathleen McCourt.
The national sample data collected in this project provided us
with a picture of Catholics after the Council and the material for
before-and-after analysis (Greeley, McCready, and McCourt
1976). In the meantime, on behalf of American bishops NORC
conducted a study of priests in the United States that I directed
with the late Richard Schoenherr, the report of which I wrote
(NORC 1972).

As I reread the results of these three studies I am astonished at
the changes reported (in the case of the 1972 study of priests, as
measured by retrospective questions). A tremendous amount had
changed in a very short period of time, enough for me to conclude now that the "effervescence" of what can properly be called
a Catholic revolution had worked its destabilization on the
Church in a very short time and had already spent its force by the
time NORC conducted its first General Social Survey in 1972.
Since then I have participated in many more studies of American
Catholics (which I will cite subsequently) that have confirmed my
conclusion that a substantial change had occurred among American Catholics. With some exceptions, however (attitudes toward
homosexuality and the ordination of women, for example), these
changes in attitudes and behavior had taken place by the mid-
1970s. The revolution I describe in this essay lasted therefore by
the most generous estimate from 1965 to 1974, and probably only
from 1966 to 1970. The revolution had occurred, the new wine
had been poured into the old wineskins, and the wineskins had
burst. Since I am an empirical sociologist, my perspective on the

state of American Catholicism in the past four decades has been shaped by these research projects, which provide the raw material for this essay.

For many years I was unable to find a theoretical perspective with which to order these findings.[1] More recently, inspired by the work of my colleagues William Sewell Jr. and Melissa Jo Wilde, I have arrived at a theory that subsumes my data and compels me to see that a truly era-shaping revolution swept the Church between the mid-1960s and the mid-1970s, that in some respects the revolution is still going on even though the effervescence has long since gone out of it, and that its effects, a third of a century and two generations later, can reasonably be said to be permanent. The theory explains what happened and points in the direction of possible responses. It has also provided hypotheses for me to test as I reexamine the work—mine and that of others— of the past four decades. If the critical issue in the revolution was the Church's right to make "rules" that everyone must obey, then one would look for explicit denial of the right to make such rules. By 1974 this right had been seriously challenged by the majority of American Catholics. They would remain Catholics on their own terms.[2] Of such denials of the legitimacy of authority are revolutions made. There are probably several reasons that I did not see this a third of a century ago. The change was so, well, revolutionary as to stun me. I was busy defending the integrity of my work from assaults on all sides. I saw what had happened and, dissatisfied as I was with those who blamed the Council for all the trauma in the Church, I did not have a theoretical perspective that explained why it had happened. Neither did anyone else.

Now I understand that the Council fathers had gleefully poured new wine into old wineskins and the wineskins had burst.

Church leaders then denied that it was new wine or that the wineskins had burst, and finally they blamed everyone else for what had happened and made no attempt to fashion new wineskins. Many of them instead called for repairing the old ones.

In addition to relying on my own data and on the theories of others that help organize them, I will perforce depend on my own experiences. I am one of the dwindling number of priests who has lived in both the Old Church and the New Church. I was there, so to speak, at the beginning of the revolution. I watched the new wine being poured and the old wineskins bursting. I heard the anxious cries of leaders saying that the old wineskins were just fine. I heard the angry, triumphant cries of the revolutionaries who stormed the Bastille (in this case, the Vatican). Foolishly, I tried to warn everyone what was happening. I grew sour when the euphoria the Council had generated ended, even if some of it had gotten out of hand. I decried foolish attempts at restoration and frivolous attempts to reduce Catholicism to low-church Protestantism. It has been my era, in the sense that it shaped much of my life (and turned me into a storyteller). One does not describe the events of one's own times from a dispassionate distance. I will try to distinguish in the course of this essay among insight gathered from experience, insight generated by data, and insight gained from the theoretical organization of my findings.

I am attempting to write a sociological history of Catholicism in the United States in the last half of the twentieth century. No person with even a smidgen of wisdom would think that such a task is possible. You cannot write a history of your own era because it's not over, and once it is, you will not be around to write it. The best one can do is report from the field, with the resources at one's command, and say what it seemed to have been like. Such an effort may provide immediacy to those who write with the perspective of later years but who weren't there. If they are wise they will at least listen to those who write with immediacy. If they don't listen, they will not understand, like most of those who now try to write about the American Catholicism of the postwar world.[3] At best, then, this essay is an interim effort.

Vatican II was an attempt at reform. No one has ever questioned the need for reform in the Church—recall the ancient dictum *ecclesia semper reformanda* (the church always needs reform). Throughout much of its history, the Church has been able to absorb various reform movements. (Its most notable failure was its inability to cope with *the* Reformation, a failure that was in part a result of the complex political situation in Europe in the sixteenth century.) In principle, reform is good. However, the usual response of Church leadership to the demand for reform is a cautious "yes, but not now." In reforms someone is bound to lose power, and no one wants to do that. Despite opposition from the Roman Curia, the Church's central bureaucracy, the Council was able to accomplish some moderate reforms. The chaos that resulted—the breaking of the old wineskins—frightened most of the Church leaders. The student unrest that swept Europe in the late 1960s also frightened them. They promptly shut down the reform movement (though the changes caused by the Council and the subsequent Catholic revolution remain, as does the chaos of split wineskins). In particular, Church leaders did not proceed with the reform of the Papacy and the Curia that should have followed the Council. As the London *Tablet* forcefully put it, they "aborted the reform."

In the following chapters, I will reflect on the kinds of behavior and policy that are appropriate for the situation that has emerged since the Council. My thesis is that the strongest resources the leadership of the Catholic Church has at its disposal are the beauty and charm of its stories. For men who are used to exercising authority and being obeyed without question, this will not be good news. To the extent that they understand my suggestions for new wineskins, they will not like them at all. Or as the Irish would say, at all, at all.

TWO

The "Confident" Church

Steven Avella (1992) called his study of the Archdiocese of Chicago during the administrations of Cardinals Samuel Stritch and
Albert Meyer (from 1940 to 1965) *This Confident Church.* I have
no disagreement with Professor Avella's book. The Church in
Chicago was surely confident, yet in retrospect the title seems unintentionally ironic. The churches in Chicago in the 1950s and
early 1960s were crowded on Sundays. The archdiocese was
opening new parishes, new grammar schools, new high schools.
Young men and women were enrolling in seminaries and novi-
tiates in large numbers. Old Catholic organizations and new ones
(the Cana Conference, the Christian Family Movement, the
Catholic Interracial Council) were flourishing. Resignations from
the priesthood and the religious life were infrequent. People
waited in long lines to go to confession every week, and in very
long lines before Easter and Christmas. Young Catholics may
have necked and petted—often to orgasm—before marriage but
usually postponed intercourse until after marriage. Husbands

and wives may have practiced birth control, but they believed it was a sin and went to confession before they received Communion or did not receive Communion until they were beyond their reproductive years. Pastors administered their parishes by sovereign right from their rectory offices, usually not feeling any need to consult anyone but their cronies. The curates did all the work and rarely argued or disagreed with pastoral decisions. The first tentative steps toward liturgical reform in new Holy Week services were successful. Catholics were attending college in large numbers; some new parishes had mostly college-educated parishioners. The children and grandchildren of immigrants had proven that they could be good Americans and good Catholics. The Church had preserved their faith. It had successfully met what it thought to be its most serious challenge: the defense of immigrant faith against destruction by a hostile Protestant culture.[1]

Yet by the end of the 1960s, these signs of vigor were disappearing. Change seemed to have dissolved them. The confident Church had been overconfident. Attendance at Mass declined sharply. Priests and nuns were leaving their vocations in large numbers—often after dating one another at the summer study weeks they attended. New vocations were drying up. No new parishes were founded, no new schools opened.[2] Young men and women were beginning to cohabit before marriage. Married people were practicing birth control, often with the approval of their priests, and not confessing it. Curates were challenging the divine right of pastors, many of whom were being forced into retirement. The laity were telling the clergy how to run their parishes, as though that was their right. The old "movements" carefully controlled by "downtown" had lost their influence and were being replaced by radical "peace and justice" movements. The confident Church was disintegrating.[3]

The confidence of the previous years had assumed that nothing in the Church would or could change. The archdiocese did not take into account the possibility of change that would shatter the ecclesiastical structures that underpinned its confidence.[4] It was in fact utterly unprepared for change—as was the rest of Catholic Christianity. Nothing much had changed in Catholicism for almost two centuries. Why should one worry about the impact of change?

For much of the nineteenth and twentieth centuries, the Catholic Church had organized itself to resist the Enlightenment and the French Revolution. It proudly denounced science, rationality, and democracy as godless. It categorically rejected the modern world, whatever "modern" might have meant at any given time. It excommunicated, silenced, or denounced any of its own members who were even slightly inclined to consider the theories of the French Revolution. It allied itself solidly with the Old Regime against "liberals," "republicans," "secularists," and "moderns." It absolutely forbade the use of techniques of literary criticism on the Bible. It piled up condemnations in the Index of Forbidden Books. It defined papal infallibility in the teeth of internal questioning and external ridicule. It could not and would not consider any compromise with the enemies beyond its gates. There could be no ecumenism with Protestants.[5] Jews were denounced on Good Friday as "perfidious." Jews (and Masons) were also thought to be the principal leaders in liberal attacks on the Church. Pagan babies should be ransomed so that their souls would be saved. It condemned Marx, Darwin, and Freud and forbade Catholics to read them. Evolution was unacceptable if it implied any development of the human soul.

In retrospect, this style of Catholicism seems mindless. Did the Church really expect to survive the changes brought about by science and democracy and reason without altering itself in any way? The only answer is that it was utterly certain that it could. It may have been a beleaguered garrison under attack from all sides, but it had been in that position before and had survived; it would, with God's grace, do the same again. Moreover, if only the modern world would listen, Catholicism had the answers to all its problems, answers deduced from its traditional philosophical principles. The world would eventually learn that the Church was right and it was wrong. In the historical context in which the Church found itself after the Congress of Vienna and before World War II, such an orientation did not seem at all unreasonable. (Nor does it seem unreasonable today to those, many of them architects of the Council, who see the same enemies lurking all around.)

Enlightenment rationalism, unlike modern agnosticism, was vehemently atheistic. God and the Church were the enemies and should be destroyed. The royal houses of Europe, for reasons of their own, fended off these assaults until 1789, though they strove (like Emperor Joseph II of Austria) to make the Church as dependent on them as Peter I had in Russia and Henry VIII had in England. Then the French Revolution, to an extent that most contemporary Catholics do not understand, went about the destruction of the Church. Bishops, priests, and nuns were killed, churches and monasteries sacked, lands confiscated, religious schools closed, Rome occupied—and the pope died a prisoner in France.

Always the pragmatist, Napoléon Bonaparte decided that the Church could be useful to him as long as it did what he told it to do. He dragged the new pope to Paris to officiate at his coronation and took the crown from the pope's hands and placed it on his own head. The Church in France (and in the various occupied countries) was but a shadow of what it had been. Many enlightened folk (especially in England) firmly believed that Pius VII would be the last pope and the Catholic Church would simply fade away. It had been discredited and demolished.

However, they did not reckon with the historic resilience of Catholicism. After Waterloo and the Congress of Vienna, the Papacy hunkered down in the shrunken papal states, tried to fight off the various republican and liberal and Modernist attacks of the next century, and stirred up the faith and devotion of its laypeople. It was astonishingly successful because many Europeans still liked being Catholic and were happy to have the churches open again and priests in them. Old religious orders (even the disbanded Jesuits) were restored, new orders were founded, missionaries were sent forth, old devotions were revived and new ones (like Lourdes) celebrated. Men and women entered the priesthood and the religious life (then a risky choice) in considerable numbers. Monasteries were rebuilt, schools reopened, libraries restocked. The laity flocked to the Church in large numbers. The Enlightenment and the Revolution had misread the strength of religious faith among the peasantry.

Heartened by the religious revival of the first half of the nineteenth century, the Church saw no reason to lower the walls of its garrison fortress to allow in science or democracy or enlightenment. Moreover, its enemies were still attacking. Clergy were murdered by the Paris Communes of 1848 and 1870 (often in the square of Notre Dame). The liberal governments that came to power promptly renewed their attacks on the clergy and on Church schools. Monasteries were closed again and priests and nuns once again turned out to fend for themselves. Most religious orders were banned again in France at the beginning of the twentieth century. It was necessary that the Church resist these assaults on its rights and protect the faith of the ordinary simple laity.[6]

In addition, the independence of the Church was under constant threat from revolutionary attempts to create a united Italy. If the Piedmontese could take over Rome, then the Church would be utterly dependent on the House of Savoy, which had allied itself with the liberals.[7] The Papacy could hardly be expected to approve an Italian nationalism that had murdered the pope's prime minister before his eyes in the Piazza del San Pietro. Catholic leaders, with little dissent from ordinary Catholics, believed that the struggle would go on for a long time. The Church would never yield to its enemies, even when the pope retreated to the Vatican palace. Slowly but surely, structures of opposition, resistance, and negation came to form the modes of Catholic life. The garrison Church had hardened into a kind of permanent fortress. It would not change; it could not change.

On the face of it, that argument cannot stand up to the historical evidence. The journey from the Upper Room in Jerusalem to the Vatican, the Roman Curia, and canon law has been a long and complex one. Interest on loans was once denounced as usury. Slavery was once defended. The Papacy was corrupt for centuries. Priests had de facto wives, as did bishops. Catholics received the sacrament of penance only twice in life. Many (including St. Thomas Aquinas) thought that laity could give absolution.

A fetus was thought to become human only after the third month of pregnancy. Heliocentrism was once rejected. The Church replaced Platonic philosophy with Aristotelian philosophy. The premise of an utterly changeless Church is absurd.

However, under constant attack and driven by the need to protect the faith of ordinary people, the Church worked on the pragmatic assumption that talk of change at this particular time in history was treason. Catholicism may have at one time embraced Platonic philosophy, at another the folk religions of the Germanic tribes (through Gregory the Great), the odd monastic practices of the Irish, Aristotelian philosophy as served up by Spanish Arabs, the militant faith of the knightly military orders, Renaissance humanism, the Baroque in art and architecture. It had also embraced the positive dimensions of every culture it had encountered (at least on some occasions). For a millennium it had presided over artistic development in music, painting, architecture, poetry, and sculpture. Could it not have in principle found some aspects of modernity with which, to use a word that was a long time coming, to dialogue?

The answer to that in the post–French Revolution Church was a flat no. In the Pastoral Constitution on the Church in the Modern World, the fathers of the Council said yes—and have been the object of attacks by many second-guessers ever since.

There were many Catholic scholars and leaders during this long era of intransigence who sometimes gently and sometimes forcefully argued for adaptation—in the nineteenth century, Rosmini-Serbati, Lammenais, Lacordaire, Montalembert, Newman, and Acton, among others.[8] In the twentieth century, Joseph Lagrand, Maurice Blondel, Henri de Lubac, Jean Daniélou, Yves Congar, Pierre Teilhard de Chardin, and John Courtney Murray were silenced or sent into exile or forbidden to teach or write.[9] Their ideas were perhaps not heretical, but they were considered dangerous both because they might shock the faithful and because they might encourage the Church's enemies (communists, socialists, secularists, Protestants, Jews).

It is beyond the purposes of this essay to discuss the assault on the Church from the Enlightenment to the present. It is at least arguable, however, that clericalism tends to generate anticlericalism.

A more pertinent question might be whether there was a time when the defensive strategy could have been reevaluated. Before the Great War? The fierce anticlericalism of France's Third Republic, as well as the wholesale condemnation of the Modernist controversy, made change at that time impossible, though the Church probably could have made some changes at that time. After the Great War? Europe was exhausted, but many theologians who had fought in the war were convinced that Protestantism was no longer a threat. If Pope Benedict XV had lived longer, some attempts might have been made to ease the tension between the Catholic Church and everyone else. The establishment of Vatican City might have been an occasion for that. The Malines conversations between a Belgian cardinal and Anglicans could have gone further than they did. Anticlericalism, for all its venom in France and its murders in Spain, was perhaps on the wane. However, communism had become an ominous threat, as had the emergence of Nazism in Germany—hardly times to lower the garrison walls or let the enemy, or those sympathetic to the enemy, in the gates.

Could the strategy have been reevaluated after 1945, a time of great intellectual and scholarly ferment in the Church (which was not the case after 1918)? Perhaps. Pius XII wrote an encyclical on the Bible in the 1940s that encouraged Catholic scholars to use the new methods of analysis to understand what the authors really meant. He also encouraged the liturgical revival that attempted to increase active lay participation in the Church's worship. Both the encyclical and the liturgical revival would become very important at the Council. However, worried by the ferment, Pius XII also issued in 1950 an encyclical that squelched the new theological discussions and silenced many of the Church's most gifted scholars—men who would later shape the Council. The great enemies—secularism and communism and false ecumenism—were too strong for the Church to run the risk of change, even though it began to appear that the old struggle between the Church and the French Revolution was dissolving in the atmosphere of postwar prosperity and the stern benignity of *le général*.

These questions are of course unanswerable. However, as one looks back, one can't help but wonder if the new wine would have had a less destructive impact on the old wineskins if it had been poured more slowly earlier in the twentieth century.

Most of us humans are aware only dimly, if at all, of the structures that shape our lives. Most early-twentieth-century Catholics did not know that what they presumed had always been the style of the Church had evolved in a century-long struggle with the French Revolution. They did know that there was an elaborate complex of rules they had to obey to be a "practicing Catholic" or a "Catholic in good standing." They had to attend Mass every Sunday. They could be late for Mass but not too late. They could not eat meat on Friday. They could not eat or drink after midnight if they wished to receive Holy Communion, not even a sip of water if they came home at 12:01. They could not marry someone who was not Catholic. If they insisted on doing so and could not pressure the prospective spouse into converting, they had to marry in the rectory parlor and only after extracting promises from the partner that were a violation of the partner's rights. They had to fast during Lent and on certain other days of the year. In addition to Sunday, there were certain other Holy Days of Obligation on which they had to go to Mass "under pain of mortal sin."[10]

They could not divorce, they could not practice birth control, they were not supposed to attend "condemned" films or read "forbidden" books. They could not participate in Protestant or Jewish services. They ought not attend non-Catholic universities (though that was not strictly forbidden). They should abstain from all sexual pleasure during courtship, save for an occasional very chaste kiss or affectionate touch—the latter never in the wrong places. They should contribute to the support of their pastor. They should avoid all serious "occasions of sin"—like dating a divorced person or reading *Playboy*. They should not do "servile work" on Sunday. They should marry in the parish of the bride and accept the pastor's decision about whether an "outside" priest could preside over the ceremony. Under no circumstances could a woman have an abortion, even if she might die as a result of pregnancy or childbirth. Catholics should not marry before a Protestant minister or a justice of the peace; indeed, they were "excommunicated" if they should try. They should not seek "artificial" help in becoming pregnant. They should not have doubts about God or their faith. They should not permit "dirty thoughts" in their minds and should certainly not enjoy them. Young women should dress modestly—and there were organizations that would provide measurements for acceptable hemlines. Et cetera, et cetera, et cetera.

Those were the rules. If you wanted to be a good Catholic you kept the rules. If you didn't keep them, you weren't a good Catholic. Rules were what Catholicism was all about. People tended to keep the rules because they wanted to be Catholic. Why did they put up with such a rule-dominated religion? There was, they seemed to sense, more to Catholicism than the rules, though the rules were what they heard about all the time. There were the Mass and the Sacraments, Mary the mother of Jesus, the saints and the angels and the souls in purgatory, the warmth and color of the church with the tabernacle light burning in the sanctuary and the statues and the stained glass windows, May crownings, First Communions, confirmations, grammar school graduations, the consolation of the Requiem Mass, the sense of parish community—the place you said you came from when asked, the high club dances, the basketball and volleyball courts, the softball leagues, the wise and kindly priest and the gentle and sympathetic nun (though neither of these seemed to be a majority), the friends and neighbors—all the things about Catholicism that really mattered and for which keeping the rules was a price you had to pay.

There were exceptions and exemptions and dispensations. You could, for example (even without a dispensation), eat meat on Friday if a refusal to do so would embarrass your hostess. You could miss Mass on Sunday if you had a long trip or a vacation (or even more than a half hour's drive or when you traveled on an airplane, according to some casuists). Most people tried to get to Mass anyway, because they were Catholics and Catholics went to Mass on Sunday. There were various canonical exemptions that made divorce possible. You could also get an "annulment," though it was very difficult. Some people even knew about "internal" forum solutions to marriage problems. Priests could give you permission to read certain books (though not to look at *Playboy!*).

There was even a way around the birth control rule. In the seminary we were told that if one spouse insisted on contraceptive intercourse, the other spouse could accept that and continue engaging in intercourse for the sake of preserving the marriage. The accepting partner, however, could not initiate intercourse.[11] We were warned not to tell people about this exception; apparently they didn't have the right to know it. A lot of problems would have been solved if we had told them.

You could brush your teeth or take medicine after midnight even if you wanted to receive Communion. Less than an ounce of meat did not break the rule of Friday abstinence, nor did forgetful eating of meat. However, if you remembered halfway through a meal that it was Friday, you had to stop eating. There was also a wonderfully consoling doctrine called *epikeia* that meant that you could excuse yourself from some rules if you had solid reason to believe that, under the circumstances, the lawgiver would not insist that you keep them. However, the laity were warned against dispensing or excusing themselves; better always to ask a priest. Even if you wanted to practice the rhythm method of contraception, you were to ask permission—which sometimes was refused.

Not knowing about the threats of Enlightenment anticlericals or Revolutionary liberals, Catholics did not understand where all these rules came from in a Church purportedly founded by a man who opposed rule-driven religion. Nonetheless, the rules were always there. They were part of being Catholic, and most Catholics accepted them, if not always without question. Many kept them most of the time, others failed to keep them and felt guilt. Some bluntly rejected them but remained nominal Catholics. Still others, particularly creative artists, simply left the Church—writers like James T. Farrell, John O'Hara, Scott Fitzgerald. Others, including filmmakers Frank Capra, John Ford, and Martin Scorcese, did not.

In the mid–twentieth century, the clergy who imposed the rules and dispensed from them (or on occasion found ways around them) were no longer threatened by Voltaire or Robespierre or the Paris Communards. However, they felt that enforcement of the rules was important in order to protect the faith of often illiterate immigrants. Catholicism had, so to speak, two faces—the one of Sacrament and celebration and community, the other of rules and enforcement.

There were some problems with this rule-oriented religious style. For one thing, there was little nuance among the rules. Abortion was a mortal sin; so was eating meat on Friday. Intercourse with your affianced was a mortal sin; so was receiving Communion after taking a drink of water. Marrying a divorced person was a mortal sin; so was mowing your lawn on Sunday. The rules were bound together in a tight network. If you changed one of them, confidence in the other rules might falter. If you permitted someone to escape the rule on reading Freud, then he might also dismiss the rule on playing with the body of his date. All the rules hung together—not logically or theologically, but psychologically, in the minds of those who were forced to keep them, so that if the one changed, the whole ball of wax would disintegrate.

Moreover, while there were reasons behind the rules, the matter often finally came down to a blunt "This is what the Church (or the pope) says." You do it because we tell you to do it. We always have. We always will. Educated Catholics in a free society could have more insistently demanded better explanations, but as of the mid-twentieth century, that had not yet happened.

Finally, there was little room in a rule-driven Catholicism for middle ground between what was forbidden and what was permitted. You couldn't eat meat on Friday and that was that. Then the rules began to change and Catholics heard, well, you can eat meat on Friday, but you should voluntarily do other forms of penance. The laity didn't know from voluntary; they engaged in prescribed rituals of self-denial because they had to. They had no experience in making up their own rituals. Their identity was tied to obligatory fish on Friday. How did you establish a new, freely chosen identity? "You have to go to Mass on Sunday and that's that" is clear enough. But was does it mean to say "You ought to go to Mass on Sunday to express your Catholic convictions"? Once the rules are repealed, either by those in authority or by yourself, are there any other norms or standards you might want to follow? Maybe Catholics should avoid meat on Friday not for fear of sin but to assert a Catholic identity? What did that mean?

This, then, in brief summary, was the "confident" Church on the eve of the Second Vatican Council, when I began my sociological monitoring of American Catholicism—Catholicism, one might say, on the brink. I had already uncovered one sign that Catholicism was changing. In my doctoral dissertation, based on data from a study of 1961 college graduates, I found that Catholics were as likely to graduate from college as anyone else, and that they were likelier to go to graduate school than other Americans, especially if they had attended Catholic higher educational institutions. This contradicted a literature that had emerged in the 1950s that claimed that the intellectual failings of American

Catholics were caused by their rigid Catholic faith (see, e.g., the work of O'Dea, Ellis, Weigel, and Donovan). Most of the data on which these studies were based had been collected before World War II. After the war, supported by the G.I. Bill, young Catholics had swarmed off to college, graduate school, and careers in the arts and sciences.[12] My findings were dismissed or rejected as too optimistic, but they survived the test of future replications. Before the 1960s were over, the college graduation rate for Catholics reached 35 percent, which meant that Catholics were half again as likely to graduate from college as the average American. The days of the "immigrant Church" were coming to an end.[13]

The first Catholic school study (Greeley and Rossi 1966) confirmed this change. Half the Catholics in the sample were immigrants or children of immigrants. (In the year 2000 the proportion was 11 percent.) The other half were third- and fourth-generation. These figures, combined with the findings about college attendance, made it clear that Catholicism was poised on the edge of a dramatic change in its cultural and social context—as well as the edge of the Second Vatican Council.

No one denied that there had been a change in American Catholics between 1945 and 1960. It was obvious that Catholics were moving into the professional class. Very little thought, however, was being given to the implications of that for the rule-driven style of the Church. In 1959, those who were to speak at the annual Liturgical Conference at Notre Dame were solemnly instructed not to discuss the possibility of a vernacular liturgy lest it offend the bishops who were present. Three years later, the very same bishops voted overwhelmingly for a vernacular liturgy.

The findings of the 1963 Catholic school study confirmed the image of a confident Church. An astonishing 70 percent of those surveyed attended Mass every week; 38 percent went to confession every month, 13 percent received Holy Communion every week, 72 percent prayed privately every day, 34 percent had made a mission in the past two years, 24 percent had had a serious conversation with a priest in the past year, and 61 percent had read a Catholic newspaper or magazine. Sixty-six percent of respondents indicated they would support the priesthood as a vocational choice for their son, 60 percent the religious life for their daughter.

There was support for authority and sexual teaching—70 percent said that Jesus had made Peter and his successors, the popes, the head of the Church. Seventy-four percent said that sex when a couple were engaged was wrong, yet only 52 percent said remarriage after divorce was wrong, and 56 percent thought that birth control was always wrong. Fifty-four percent thought that the Church had the authority to teach what the proper methods of birth control were. Evaluation of clergy performance had slipped somewhat since the 1952 *Catholic Digest* study. Evaluation of sermons as "excellent" had fallen from 43 percent to 30 percent. Strongly positive ratings of the clergy as sympathetic and understanding had fallen from 72 percent to 62 percent. If there had not been so much controversy over whether the study was favorable to Catholic schools, this decline in approval of clerical performance might have stirred up some discussion. Finally, seven out of eight respondents looked forward to a liturgy that was at least partly in English.

As the confident Church edged toward the conciliar abyss, then, its people remained generally devout and supportive of authority. Birth control and divorce were troubling issues, and confidence in the performance of the clergy had ebbed somewhat, but there was little in these findings to suggest that the meetings that had started in Rome would do much to shake the structures of American Catholicism.

In this chapter I have distinguished between Catholic rules and the Catholic sense of sacramentality and community. Up to 1965, no one in the Church would have considered that distinction important. The rules *were* the Church. The other stuff was incidental. My attempts to make that distinction in the years since the Council have often been in vain. The Church is concerned that Catholics are sleeping together before marriage, practicing birth control, getting divorced, not going to Mass every Sunday—the other stuff doesn't make any difference.

The other stuff, I would argue, is the glue that has always held Catholicism together and still does, even when the wineskin bursts.

THREE

The Wineskins Burst

Between the Catholic school studies of 1963 and 1974, NORC studied the priesthood for the Catholic hierarchy, the last venture into sociology that the hierarchy would assay (NORC 1972). I shall return to this study in subsequent chapters. However, there were several items in the study that provided ominous signs for the structures of Catholicism. In the summer of 1968, after a papal commission recommended a change in birth control teaching, Pope Paul VI issued the encyclical *Humanae vitae*, which rejected the recommendations of the commission and dismissed its arguments for change. Unfortunately for the pope, the establishment of the commission and the subsequent leaking of its majority report had already created an expectation of change. Many priests in the United States (and elsewhere) were advising married men and women to make their own decisions about methods of birth control.

When the encyclical appeared, the negative reaction throughout the Catholic world was such that Pope Paul VI never wrote another, and, it is alleged, seriously considered resigning. One of the issues in the NORC study of the priesthood was whether the clergy had rallied to the pope at the time, as he had expected they would. The tool used to measure the clergy's response was a retrospective question, always a method to interpret cautiously. (See tables 1–3.)

The findings were that instead of increasing their opposition to artificial birth control in response to the pope's decision, priests were now likelier to be tolerant of it and less likely to refuse absolution to those who would not promise to give it up. Whether or not they remembered accurately their practice in previous years, the important fact was that the majority of priests were no longer ready to enforce the ban on artificial birth control by denying absolution. Given the almost universal insistence on the ban before 1963, this decision by priests strongly suggested that the rules structure of the Church was in serious trouble.[1] The change was abrupt and, it seemed, decisive. Moreover, only among priests over the age of fifty-five were the majority now convinced that masturbation was always a serious sin (see table 3).

These findings were so shattering that the only possible reaction among Church leadership was denial. How could priests have changed their minds so drastically only a few years after the Council? Hence there was no preparation for the results revealed four years later, when the second Catholic school study made it possible to measure lay attitudes and behavior before and after the Council.

According to the 1974 study, American Catholics strongly endorsed the Second Vatican Council (Greeley, McCready, and Mc-Court 1976). Sixty-seven percent thought its changes were for the better (and only 19 percent thought they were for the worse).

Table 1. *Attitudes of Priests toward Birth Control before and after 1968 Encyclical*

	Five years ago	Today
Always morally wrong	40%	29%
Laity must obey Church stance	11%	11%
Some methods morally acceptable with good reason	15%	13%
Some methods morally acceptable, others wrong	5%	4%
Decision should be left to conscience of laity	22%	32%
All methods morally acceptable	5%	7%
Other	2%	3%

SOURCE: NORC 1972.

Table 2. *Confessional Practice regarding Birth Control Use*

	Five years ago	Today
Deny absolution to users	26%	13%
Discourage use but not deny absolution to users	36%	33%
Accept moral judgment of responsibly formed conscience of users	31%	44%
Encourage users who have adequate reason	5%	7%
Other	2%	2%

SOURCE: NORC 1972.

Table 3. *Attitudes of Priests toward Masturbation, by Age*

	Age of priests			
	26–35	*36–45*	*46–55*	*Over 55*
Viewed as normal developmental stage	64%	52%	36%	15%
Viewed as no more than venially sinful	20%	23%	25%	21%
Viewed as mortal sin	12%	17%	32%	59%
Other	4%	8%	7%	5%

SOURCE: NORC 1972.

More than four out of five approved of the new vernacular liturgy. Two out of three supported the guitar Mass, lay clothes for nuns, and "progressive" religious education. A little less than half liked the "handshake of peace" at Mass. Fears that change would offend the laity did not seem to have been justified.

Yet as Table 4 shows, changes in attitudes and behavior during the years since the previous Catholic school study (Greeley and Rossi 1966) had been dramatic, if not to say traumatic. Weekly Mass attendance had fallen by 20 percent, monthly confession by 21 percent, and attendance at a parish mission by 28 percent. Only half the Catholic population believed with certainty that missing Mass on Sunday through one's own fault was a mortal sin. Only 17 percent thought that remarriage after divorce was always wrong (a decline from 52 percent). Sixteen percent believed that contraception was always wrong (a decline from 56 percent). Seventy-two percent believed that abortion should be legal if the child would be born severely handicapped. Support for the

Church's right to teach what books were immoral declined 27 percent, and support for its right to teach about acceptable means of birth control went down 22 percent. Only 23 percent rated sermons as "excellent." The proportion that felt they would be happy if a son chose to be a priest diminished from 66 percent to 50 percent. The proportion of income contributed to the Church fell by almost half, from 2.2 percent to 1.7 percent. Belief that Jesus had made Peter and his successors, the popes, head of the Church had declined by 28 percent. Only a third believed with certainty that the pope was infallible in faith and morals. Nevertheless, only 14 percent said that they had ever thought of leaving the Church.

However, the weekly reception of Holy Communion had increased, doubling from 13 percent to 26 percent. Less than one-fifth of those who had attended Mass every week had received Communion in 1963, as opposed to half of those who attended weekly in 1974. One angry critic of this finding shouted, "They're in a state of mortal sin!" A more reasoned answer might have been that a decade previous they might have thought they were, but they didn't any more.

The numbers in table 4 were astonishing a quarter of a century ago. Today they are equally if not more astonishing. They represent what is probably the most drastic change in Catholic attitudes and behavior in the history of the Church—and all in the wake of an ecumenical council of which most Catholics enthusiastically approved![2]

Moreover, the situation depicted in table 4 did not improve between 1974 and 2000.[3] Disapproval of birth control fell by another 4 percent, to 12 percent. Tolerance of legal abortion in cases where the child would be severely handicapped inched up to

Table 4. *Changes in Attitudes and Behavior of Catholics between 1963 and 1974*

	1963	1974
Attend mass weekly	70%	50%
Attend confession monthly	38%	17%
Pray daily	72%	60%
Receive communion weekly	13%	26%
Have attended a parish mission within past year	34%	6%
Have read a Catholic paper within past week	61%	56%
Believe sex before marriage is always wrong	74%	35%
Have had a conversation with a priest within past year	24%	20%
Believe missing Mass is a sin		53%
Have thought of leaving Church		14%
Believe Jesus made Peter and popes head of Church	70%	42%
Believe pope is infallible		32%
Believe sex for pleasure alone is acceptable	29%	50%
Believe remarriage after divorce is wrong	52%	17%
Believe contraception is always wrong	56%	16%
Believe legal abortion acceptable if child would be handicapped		72%
Accept Church's right to teach what books are immoral	87%	60%
Accept Church's right to teach about acceptable birth control	54%	32%
Would support decision of son to be a priest	66%	50%
Rate sermons as excellent	30%	23%
Rate priests' level of sympathy as excellent	62%	48%
Percent of income contributed to Church	2.2%	1.7%

SOURCE: Greeley, McCready, and McCourt 1976.

80 percent. Approval of priestly sympathy fell by half, as did the percentage of those who thought premarital sex was always wrong. Contributions to the Church fell to around 1 percent of income. Attitudes about homosexuality also shifted, so that by 2000 the majority of Catholics did not think it was always wrong. As the issues of in utero and in vitro fertilization arose, Catholic couples simply ignored the Church's prohibitions. Church attendance stabilized in the 1970s (Hout and Greeley 1987) but more recently slipped to 42 percent attending at least two or three times a month.

The old wineskins had burst.[4]

FOUR

What Happened?

What happened between the end of the Council and the 1974 study?[1] Some blamed the temper of the country in the late 1960s. A youth culture had spawned drug abuse, rock and roll music, sexual promiscuity, and disrespect for authority. This culture had infiltrated the Church and was responsible for the catastrophic change in Catholic belief and practice. Such a view, however, cannot stand up to analysis that shows that the change in sexual attitudes occurred in every age cohort, not just the young. Even those in their sixties changed their minds about birth control, divorce, and premarital sex.

The Council was an obvious target for those who thought there might be some truth in the numbers in table 4. Before the Council, a vigorous Church dominated an obedient and faithful people who kept the rules. After the Council? Confusion, chaos, and rebellion. Answer? The Council was to blame! Pope John was a senile fool! The theologians who ran it were radicals, possibly communist agents! Undo the Council! Go back to the Church of rules and mortal sin!

Such advice is like telling the cowboy whose prize stallion has escaped to lock the gate of his corral. More moderate Catholics might also say that such a policy suggested that the Holy Spirit must have abandoned the Church in the 1960s, for the bishops of the world, in ecumenical council and approved by the pope, to be so profoundly mistaken.[2] A revised version of the same argument, still popular in some quarters (not excluding the Vatican), is that Pope John was a saintly man who didn't know quite what he was doing and Pope Paul a victim of vacillation who could not make decisions. The theological advisers did not understand sound Catholic doctrine as well as they might have. It is therefore necessary to restore the Catholic tradition as best one can, by emphasizing the continuity of the Council with the past; to modify some of the changes that have occurred since then; and to gradually restore the old discipline. No one who embraced this model, as far as I am aware, explained the dynamics by which the Council caused the decline in religious practice. The argument was generally *post-hoc, ergo propter-hoc:* the changes occurred after the Council, therefore the Council caused them.

The argument was popular with the revisionists and restorationists whose work prior to the Council had influenced it and whose presence as advisers helped shape it, men such as Jean Daniélou, Henri de Lubac, Hans Urs von Balthasar, Joseph Ratzinger, and the philosopher Jacques Maritain. They turned their backs on their own work, usually without the grace to admit that they were responsible for it.

In the report on the 1974 Catholic school study (Greeley, Mc-

Cready, and McCourt 1976), I proposed a model that linked the changes to the birth control encyclical. After the Council and until 1968, Church attendance had *increased*. If one took into account changing attitudes on sex and authority, one could account for all the other declines—attendance at Mass, confession, contributions, support for vocations. I still think that model is useful, but that the dynamics of the change must be explicated more carefully.

There are two major tendencies in interpretation of the Second Vatican Council. The first, which dominated the Vatican at the end of the second millennium, is that the Council was an *occurrence*, a meeting of the bishops of the world, who enacted certain reforms and clarified certain doctrines. It was therefore an exercise in continuity and not in change; the response and clarification were necessary but they did not drastically change the nature of the Church. To find out what this occurrence, the "Council rightly understood" of Cardinal Joseph Ratzinger, meant, one must go to the conciliar documents. The second interpretation holds that the Council was a momentous *event*, indeed one of the most dramatic and important events in the history of Catholicism, a structure-shattering event one could almost call a revolution.

I began to ponder this debate after a conversation with a senior American prelate. He had remarked that the American bishops had made serious mistakes in their implementation of the Council, but that they could not be blamed because they had never had to implement a council before. I agreed, though I thought to myself I probably meant something different than he did. I thought he might have meant that they should have proceeded more slowly and cautiously, while I meant that they should not have tried to make so many changes in the Church while asserting all along that nothing was changing.

Then I discovered in the work of my friend and colleague Professor William Sewell, Jr., a model of social historical analysis (see Sewell 1992). It made me rethink the Council and what it did and didn't do. The Council was, in fact, *both* an occurrence and an event. It is folly to pretend that the event did not occur or that it can be undone. To understand Catholicism today, one must recognize what has happened and work from there. I must note here that I wrote some time ago that with or without the Council, the same changes would have occurred. Looking back on that statement, I must admit that it was not the most intelligent sentence I ever put on paper. No one knows what would have happened. But the fact is that there was a Council (presumably in Catholic doctrine inspired by the Holy Spirit), and the Church did go through enormous change. One must therefore strive to describe what happened.

Sewell, who has a joint appointment at the University of Chicago in history and political science, is concerned with structures and events, patterns of behavior and historical shifts that drastically reshape those patterns. He does not believe in "social laws," inexorable historical processes that direct the progress of human events. He writes, "Sociology's epic quest for social laws is illusory, whether the search is for timeless truths about all societies, ineluctable trends of more limited historical epochs, or inductively derived laws of certain classes of social phenomena. Social processes are inherently contingent, discontinuous, and open-ended" (Sewell 1996).

Sewell thus rejects the historical models of Weber, Durkheim,

Marx, Comte, and all the others who find inexorable trends in human events, including implicitly those who babble today about postmodernism. His description of what actually happens in the "buzzing, blooming pluralism" of the human condition may seem like common sense, but it goes against what many sociologists and most pop sociologists believe. For the purposes of this essay, it also goes against the vague intellectualism of many Catholic commentators who think they can discern the secrets of history and summarize them in a couple of clear and simple paragraphs.

"Adequate eventful accounts of social process will look more like well-made stories or narratives than like laws of physics," argues Sewell. He uses what Robert Merton calls "middle-range" theories to account for contingent phenomena to determine why contingent events (about which there was no inevitability) have such important and sometimes momentous impact on the structures of human existence.

Sewell is also concerned with the "structures" of human behavior, that is, the *routine* patterns of human action. A structure, according to Sewell, is "the tendency of patterns of relationships to be reproduced even when actors engaging in the relations are unaware of the patterns or do not desire their reproduction." In contrast, an "event" is a series of historical occurrences that results in the durable transformation of structures. There are two dimensions of a structure, the *schema*—pattern itself—and *resources*—the motivations and constraints that reinforce the schema and are in turn reinforced by it. Think of Catholics and the obligation of Sunday Mass: it was routine behavior, not explicitly reflected upon, carried out routinely because it was part of being Catholic and it would be a mortal sin to omit it. Sewell, who is not Catholic, gives another illustration: "The priest's power to consecrate the host derives from schemas operating at two rather different levels. First, a priest's training has given him mastery of a wide range of explicit and implicit techniques of knowledge and self-control that enable him to perform satisfactorily as a priest. And second, he has been raised to the dignity of the priesthood by an ordination ceremony that, through the laying on of hands by a bishop, has mobilized the power of apostolic succession and thereby made him capable of an apparently miraculous feat—transforming bread and wine into the body and blood of Christ."

Established and reinforced behavior patterns tend to be stable and durable. However, they can also change, because of external forces or internal inconsistencies within structures themselves. A wartime defeat and devastation can savage the structures of a people (though in fact, in many western European countries after 1945, it seemed that the patterned and reinforced relationships were all that remained). The "fit" between resources and schemas is not so tight that inconsistencies, uncertainties, doubts, and conflicts cannot arise, more so under some sets of circumstances than others. Ruptures may then occur in behavior patterns and motivations—a basketball team swarms off a court to protest a defeat after a referee's decision that seems unfair. Such rupture events become historical events when they "touch off a chain of occurrences that durably transforms previous structures and practices."

To paraphrase and rearrange Sewell's argument, even the accumulation of incremental changes often results in a buildup of pressure and a dramatic crisis of existing practices, rather than a gradual transition from one state of affairs to another. Lumpiness, rather than smoothness, is the normal texture of historical temporality. And while the events are sometimes the culmination of processes long under way, they typically do more than simply carry out a rearrangement of practices made necessary by gradual and cumulative social change. Historical events tend to transform social relations in ways that could not be fully predicted from the gradual changes that may have made them possible. What makes historical events so important is that they reshape history by imparting an unforeseen direction to social development.

Events, then, should be conceived of as sequences of occurrences that result in the transformation(s) of structures. Such sequences begin with a rupture of some kind—that is, a surprising break with routine practice. But whatever the nature of the initial rupture, an occurrence only becomes a historical event when it touches off a chain of occurrences that durably transforms previous structures and practices.

Sewell's example of such a structure-shattering event is the storming of the Bastille in Paris in July 1789. Paris was on the edge that summer. The crown had run out of money. The Estates General had convened and constituted itself as a National Assembly, and King Louis dismissed the liberal minister Necker, surrounded Paris with troops, and seemed ready to suppress the National Assembly. Underlying the growing tensions between the king and his supporters and the Enlightenment-influenced National Assembly was a sharp division over the nature of sovereignty. Prospects for the harvest seemed poor. Pamphlets and newspapers were flooding Paris with incendiary articles. Mobs ransacked the city.

On the morning of July 14, representatives of the National Assembly government and a mob went to the Hôtel des Invalides to demand the arms that were stored there so that they could create a militia to defend the city against a possible attack by royal troops. They seized more than thirty thousand muskets and then moved to the Bastille to find gunpowder. After a bitter fight in which more than a hundred of the attackers were killed, they captured the fort, released its seven prisoners (forgers and madmen), and killed two government officials and paraded their heads around Paris on pikes.

There had been urban riots in Paris before and the battle for the Bastille was not a militarily important one, but within three days the king recalled Necker, removed the troops around Paris, and came to Paris to submit, in effect, to the wishes of the National Assembly.

At first the Assembly condemned the violence at the Bastille and indeed all political violence. But within two weeks, Sewell writes, its members had changed their minds:

> In the excitement, terror, and elation that characterized the taking of the Bastille, orators, journalists and the crowd itself seized on the political theory of popular sovereignty to explain and to justify the popular violence. This act of epoch-making cultural creativity occurred in a moment of ecstatic discovery: the taking of the Bastille, which had begun as an act of defense against the king's aggression, revealed itself in the days that followed as a concrete, unmediated, and sublime instance of the people expressing its sovereign will. What happened at the Bastille became the establishing act of revolution in the modern sense. By their action at the Bastille, the people were understood to have risen up, destroyed tyranny, and established liberty.
>
> Within a month other structure-shattering events followed: the abolition of feudal exactions, provincial and municipal privileges, exclusive hunting rights, and the confiscation and eventual sale of the vast properties of the church. The storming of the Bastille, now a culturally defined event, led to the utter transformation of the structures of French so-

ciety in an outburst of exuberant creativity. The Old Regime would linger on at least till 1830 in one fashion or another. But the New Regime had in fact replaced it.

Would the political and social development of the (then) largest and most powerful country in Europe have been different if that event had not occurred? Did there have to be a revolution and then the bloody wars that lasted until 1815 and struggles in the twentieth century up to 1945? Was the development on balance good or bad? Might a more peaceful evolutionary transformation of power have been less traumatic for France? There are many different answers to these questions, and indeed the politics of France for two centuries have been, in part, a battle between those who accept the Revolution and those who in some sense do not. But the important point in Sewell's analysis is that the storming of the Bastille, once interpreted as a revolutionary, momentous event, shattered and eventually replaced the social, political, and religious structures of France.

I now propose to apply Sewell's model to Vatican II, and to argue that while the Council's various documents, taken singly or together, were not, in and of themselves, the cause of the shattering of structures in the Catholic Church, the Council, as (irrevocably) interpreted, was, in addition to and beyond its decisions, a historical *event* of enormous importance for the Church.

I will consider three structures of twentieth-century Catholicism that shaped the Catholic institution: the centralization of power in the Vatican; the post-Tridentine understanding of sin; and the conviction that the Church is the immutable. Prior to Vatican II, it was assumed that decision making flowed downward, and that those who disagreed with the pope or any higher Church leaders were no longer Catholic. It was further assumed that the primary goal of a good Catholic was the salvation of his or her soul, a goal that could be attained by avoiding sins and keeping all the rules (which were de facto the same thing), or, once sins were committed, by confessing them in species and number. It was finally assumed that the Church could not change, had not changed, and would never change. These "schemas," reinforced by such "resources" as theories of the divine origin of the Church and papal infallibility, set the parameters of Catholicism inside the worldviews of the Counter-Reformation, the centralization of papal power at the First Vatican Council, and the condemnation of Modernism at the beginning of the twentieth century.

It might have been true that pluralistic decisions about power had been characteristic of the Church for many centuries (for example, in the internal governance of some religious orders). It might have been true that in its long history the Catholic Church had often changed (most recently on such issues as slavery and coeducation). It might have been true that one ceases to be a Catholic not when one disagrees with the pope but only when one joins another church or formally and explicitly renounces the faith. Finally, it might have been true that the central truth of Christianity was God's forgiving love, which Christians were to imitate. Nonetheless, in the minds of most of the laity and the clergy and those who were not Catholic, Catholicism before Vatican II was in fact a centralized, immutable, and sin- and rule-driven heritage. Most of the bishops who attended the Council came to Rome fully accepting those assumptions.

On the surface, the Catholic Church in 1962 was not nearly as edgy as the populace of Paris in 1789. Yet Pope Pius XII, the predecessor of Pope John XXIII, who would convene the Council, had instigated changes during his long administration that might, in retrospect, seem seditious. He approved changes in the liturgy of Holy Week, the modern critical study of the Bible, and, in effect, birth control, by accepting the rhythm method. A new emphasis on the Mystical Body of Christ, the teaching that the laity, as well as the pope and the bishops, was in some fashion the Church, suggested to small groups of laity that perhaps the Church ought to listen to them. Scholars, digging into the liturgical, theological, and organizational history of the Church, found a much more variegated Catholicism than the existing official structure of immutable centralization indicated. Bishops, however conservative, did not like the heavy-handed behavior of the curial dicasteries. An increasingly well-educated Catholic laity was uneasy with the rigidity of the Church. Married people found the birth control teaching difficult, a teaching that became a matter of heavy emphasis only after 1930 (Noonan 1965). Parish priests were increasingly uneasy with the apparent insensitivity of the Church to the problems of the laity, and the "Catholic Action" movements were producing cadres of well-informed, dedicated laypeople. Finally, the disaster of World War II and the surprising rebirth of Europe following the war created an atmosphere in which many Catholics felt that some modifications in the Church's various stances might be appropriate. None of these events, separately or in combination, seemed then to have constituted a prerevolutionary situation. In retrospect, they can be seen as the raw material for drastic change; in Sewell's terms, the resources for new structures.

Nonetheless, there were signs of slippage. As I have noted, by

1963, half of the Catholics in America did not think birth control was always wrong, and studies showed that most American Catholic women practiced some kind of contraception before the end of their fertility. Still, many, if not most, probably confessed to their use of birth control. Moreover, the Catholic hierarchy in the United States was already bringing pressure on Rome to obtain some sort of relief for divorced and remarried Catholics, this despite the official posture that the Catholic Church could not change its teachings on marriage. Only in retrospect, however, do these issues suggest that there was serious ferment in Catholicism in the United States, or anywhere else, when Pope John convened the Council.

The Council's preparatory commissions, dominated by the Roman Curia, had prepared draft documents for the first session of the Council that would have turned it into a rubber stamp for the then existing ecclesiastical structures. Most bishops, it would seem, were prepared to vote for them and go home, still able to tell their people what they (in the bishops' minds) wanted to hear: Nothing had changed.

The occurrence that played a role something like the storming of the Bastille was the sudden opposition of two leaders of the western European Church, Cardinals Joseph Frings of Cologne and Achille Lienart of Lille.[3] At issue was the matter of voting for members of the various conciliar commissions, which would shape the documents on which the bishops would vote. The voting procedure had been slanted by the Curia. Elderly men with enormous personal prestige who had suffered through the war, Lienart and Frings demanded at the first meeting of the Council on October 13, 1962, that the Council fathers be given the opportunity to select the men who would serve on the various commissions. They requested that the voting be postponed for a single day, during which the names of men who were not on the list prepared by the Curia could be circulated. That night the pope agreed. It was clear then to at least some of the bishops that it would be their Council, not the Roman Curia's. The bishops, it turned out, had power in practice as well as in theory. The Vatican bureaucracy could be defied.[4] There was indeed a pluralism of power in the Catholic Church. As Melissa Jo Wilde observes, "The importance of Lienart's motion cannot be overstated. In the end, the elected commissions were far more diverse both ideologically and nationally than they would have been had the preparatory commission simply been re-elected. Furthermore, not only did the postponement prevent the conservatives from gaining absolute control of the conciliar commissions and eventually the very unsatisfactory preparatory constitutions from being approved, but it seems to have started a change in many of the less motivated bishops" (Wilde 2002).

On that October day, the Catholic revolution had begun. The initial battle over something so apparently minor as selecting drafting committees would change the Catholic Church forever.

That there could be pluralism of power in the Church was a very dangerous truth, as subsequent events would demonstrate. Very few Catholics, lay or clerical, realized at the time what had happened. As the Council went on, the bishops, by overwhelming votes, endorsed a broad range of changes. Joseph Komonchak has noted three overarching changes: The Council proposed a far more nuanced evaluation of the modern world; it introduced the necessity of updating and reform into the Church; and it called for greater responsibility in the local churches. The press reported, with increasing fascination and exuberance, the alteration of the unalterable.

I note five crucial changes that transformed the structures of the preconciliar Church. Here are the first three:

The liturgy. On Septuagesima Sunday, 1965, almost every altar in a Catholic church in the United States was turned around. For the first time in at least a thousand years, the priest said Mass facing the congregation, and he said it partially (soon totally) in English. If the Latin liturgy could be abandoned that easily after more than a millennium (and seven-eighths of American Catholics approved of the change), the Catholic Church could certainly change.

Ecumenism. The Council was now willing to admit that Protestant denominations were indeed churches and that Catholics should strive for mutual understanding with them in friendly dialogue. The heretics, schismatics, Jews, and infidels down the street were now suddenly separated brothers and sisters. Overnight, Catholicism was willing to change when it wanted to.

Meat on Friday. This change resulted from a decision of the American bishops after the Council was over. It may have been the most unnecessary and the most devastating. Fish on Friday had been a symbol that most visibly distinguished American Catholics from other Americans.

Bishops continued to insist that nothing had *really* changed. None of these reforms touched on the essence of Catholic doctrine. But such distinctions were lost on the laity (and on many of the clergy, too). The immutable had mutated; what would change next? When one considers the rather moderate nature of these changes, one is puzzled by the insistence that the Council caused all the subsequent trouble the Church would experience.

The centralization of authority was not yet in jeopardy, however. Change in itself did not mean that ordinary priests or laypersons could make their own decisions about the conditions under which they would be Catholic. Yet implicit in the newly discovered mutability of the Church (and in the bishops' revolt against the Curia) was the notion that if something *ought* to be changed and *would* be changed eventually, it was all right to anticipate the decision and change on one's own authority. The gradual drift in this direction in the late 1960s put the centralized authority structure of the Church in grave jeopardy.

Could the bishops have been more cautious in implementing the Council? Was the prelate I quoted above correct about the bishops' mistakes? They might have left Friday abstinence alone, but liturgical reform and ecumenism by themselves would have created a heady atmosphere in which the expectation (often eager) of more change would have swept the Church. Two subsequent developments, however, called the authority structure of the Church further into question.

Birth control. An attempt to preserve the authority structure of the Church in fact weakened and eventually came close to destroying it. There was strong sentiment among the bishops at the Council to address birth control, but Pope Paul VI, not trusting his fellow bishops with the issue, removed it from conciliar debate. Instead he appointed a special commission, which included married laypeople, to report to him on the subject. The existence of the commission became common knowledge. Laity and clergy alike assumed that if change were possible, it would occur, especially after learning that the commission had recommended change almost unanimously.

As I explained in the previous chapter, by the time the pope turned down the recommendations, the "lower orders" of the Church had already made up their minds. In terms of protecting the authority structure of the Church, it would have been better if the pope had never established the commission, or if, once it was established, he had followed its recommendation, or if he had left the matter alone. In the confusion, disappointment, and anger that followed Paul VI's *Humanae vitae* (1968), laity and clergy embraced the principle of following one's own conscience. It was this development, more than any other, that shattered the authority structure. It is often argued that priests and laypeople cannot make such decisions for themselves. Perhaps they should not, but in fact they did and do. It is further argued that they cannot be good Catholics if they make such decisions, but in fact they think they can.

This is what happens when a historical event shatters a behavior pattern and the resources that support it. The dialogue goes something like this:

"They had no right to do that!"

"But they did."

"Therefore we must force them to reverse what they did."

"That clearly is not possible. You have tried to force them for three decades now and it has not worked. You need another approach."

Unfortunately, the last sentence of the dialogue is not accepted.

In the late 1960s and early 1970s, every age segment in Catholic America changed its convictions about the legitimacy of birth control, and, more ominously, about the *right* of the Church to lay down rules for sexual behavior. Authority was no longer centralized; it had become pluralistic. Similarly, acceptance of papal infallibility fell to 22 percent of Catholics in the United States. Catholic laity, with the support of the lower clergy, had decided that it was not wrong to be Catholic on one's own terms. Such was the fruit of the Second Vatican Council—not a series of documents, but a phenomenon that transformed the behavior patterns of Catholics with regard to their Church. Catholics who decided that contraception was not wrong justified that decision by appealing not to a pope who did not understand but to a God who did. The point is not whether such a justification was proper, but that it helped to erode the mortal sin structure of preconciliar Catholicism.

Priests and nuns. A fifth critical change in the structures of the preconciliar Church was the dispensation of priests to leave the priesthood and enter ecclesiastically valid marriages, often with former nuns. This development confirmed not only the possibility of change, but the willingness of Church authorities to back down in the face of pressure.

In effect, the lower orders asked the following questions: If the Church could permit men who had left the priesthood to marry, why could it not permit them to marry while still active in the priesthood? If it could change the playing field on liturgy, ecumenism, and Friday abstinence, why not on birth control and the role of women in the Church? If so many "mortal" sins were no longer sinful, was it necessary to worry so much about sin? There are complex theological replies to these questions, but they didn't seem credible to many Catholics, who concluded, unfairly perhaps, that the Church could change whatever it wanted, if only it wanted to.

Currently, a large majority of both priests and laypeople reject the Church's official teachings on the ordination of women, birth control, premarital sex, in utero and in vitro fertilization, oral sex, and the legality of abortion under some circumstances. There is also strong movement in the direction of tolerance for homosexuality. Moreover, media surveys indicate that the laity believe that they can disagree with the pope on these issues and remain good Catholics. Central authority has lost its credibility (it has lost it on social issues like immigration, too). Thus the vigorous efforts of John Paul II to impose his teaching about the ordination of women seem to have had little effect on the attitudes of either lower clergy or laity. The structures of assent, the patterns of motivation and behavior that would have worked smoothly thirty years ago in response to such papal rulings, are simply no longer available. Catholics believe that the Church can change and that they can disregard the pope when it comes to making decisions, especially about sex and gender. Many American Catholics diminish whatever dissonance they may feel by cheering the pope when he comes to this country but ignoring what he says.

On the other hand, defection from the Church has not increased appreciably in the United States. Moreover, Catholic acceptance of such central truths as the existence of God, the divinity of Jesus, the resurrection of the dead, and the presence of Jesus in the Eucharist (however explained) has not changed. The majority of American Catholics still attend the Eucharist at least once a month.

Father John W. O'Malley S.J. summarizes neatly the paradox

of the Catholic revolution (though he doesn't call it that) in ana-
lyzing the response of Catholics to the 2002 sexual abuse crisis:

> American Catholics love their church, but it is the church
> they experience every day in the priests they know and in the
> other Catholics in the pews with them—the church as "the
> people of God," not as a hierarchical institution. It is not by
> any means that they see these two as unrelated to each other,
> but they know, quite correctly, that the second is subordinate
> to the first and has no claim to existence except to further the
> first. The church is not its ruling class.
>
> This is a distinction many Catholics could not have made
> before the council. Large numbers of Catholics at the time of
> the Reformation were in practice aware of the distinction and
> made it, dismayed though they were by the behavior of popes
> and bishops. The ecclesiology of the subsequent centuries,
> however, obscured this distinction badly, especially from the
> 19th century until the mid-20th. Critics may grieve that the
> teachings of Vatican II were never properly propagated, but
> this message about the church as a horizontal as well as a ver-
> tical reality seems to have come crashing through clear, loud
> and strong. Catholics may not be able to quote the council's
> "Dogmatic Constitution on the Church" (1964), but they got
> the point of that document: the church is defined in the first
> instance not through hierarchy and clergy, but through all its
> members, without regard to ecclesiastical status or office.
> (O'Malley 2002)

Is a restoration possible? At one time many bishops hoped that
the new *Catechism of the Catholic Church* would instruct Catholics
on what they had to believe and do, and lead to a restoration. Such
a hope was patently naïve. The twenty years of the present papal
administration have been devoted to the centralization of authority and resistance to further change. All the evidence suggests

that these efforts have had little impact. The old structures no longer exist and new, inchoate ones are in place. Thirty-five years after the Second Vatican Council, thirty of those years devoted unsuccessfully to restoration, the elimination of the structures that emerged from that historic event seems most improbable.

What is the content of the new structures, the "resources" for the new schemas, to use Sewell's term? A research project on the Catholic identity of young Catholics (Hoge et al. 2001) indicates that those under thirty are less likely to emphasize authority and sin and likelier to emphasize the presence of Christ in the Sacraments, the Real Presence, concern for the poor, and devotion to Mary the mother of God—a thoroughly Catholic identity if very different from the preconciliar identity.

Can Catholicism live with these new structures? Should it? To the first question it must be said that the Church has often in the past lived with very similar structures, indeed for much of its history. To the second I must reply that that is beyond my skills as a sociologist to judge. However, the new structures are not likely to go away. Purely from the viewpoint of a sociologist, I would suggest that perhaps the time ahead might well be a period of reconsideration and readjustment to what has become the reality of the emerging structures of contemporary Catholicism.

FIVE

"Effervescence" Spreads from the Council to the World

What happened at the Council, and subsequently, to sweep away the old structures? In her deft and brilliant study of the Council, Melissa Jo Wilde invokes a theory of collective behavior to explain the astonishing events (Wilde 2002). The tradition of collective behavior theory and research (e.g., Zald and Berger 1978 and McCarthy and Zald 1994) is impressed by the frequently observed phenomenon of the experiences of individuals merging into a group experience that is (or seems) more powerful than the sum of the individual experiences, a group experience that often overrides and even reverses the emotions the individuals bring to it and produces a mobilization of resources toward achieving the goal of the group (whether it be a religious revival or a lynching).

French sociologist Emile Durkheim, observing the religious rites of aboriginal Australians, noted how these rituals generated exuberance and joy that had not been present in individuals before the ritual and were more than the sum of individual input into the group experience. He suggested that the "effervescence" that affected the group seemed to be something that existed apart from the group. From such effervescence the notion of a distinct being—a god or God—emerged.

Most sociologists of religion think that Durkheim's explanation of how gods appeared is at best incomplete. However, no one denies the presence or the power of effervescence in human actions. For the purposes of this essay, I need not go into detail on the various explanations for the phenomenon of collective effervescence. Wilde's application of the theory to the Council and her retrieval of Durkheim's concept of effervescence (which much of the current literature on collective behavior seems to have forgotten) is a major contribution to both the sociology of religion and the sociology of collective behavior. She contends that the fathers of the Council were caught up in collective behavior of the most extraordinary kind. An archive of interviews with bishops Wilde examined is quite explicit about the hope and euphoria that swept through them at the Council. Despite their initial expectations that nothing would happen at the meetings, they began (after the interventions of Frings and Lienart) to realize that the Church could change, was changing, and that they were going to change it. Heady new wine!

Wilde quotes a letter from Cardinal Lecaro: "I certainly never felt so absorbed into the church of God as I did today. . . . All this made me feel the vitality of the church, its unity and variety together, its humanity and its divinity; it created within me, who felt myself a member of it invested with special functions and powers, a deep feeling of joy and gratitude to the Lord."[1] Wilde then quotes Durkheim: "The very act of congregating is an exceptionally powerful stimulant. Once the individuals are gathered together, a sort of electricity is generated from their closeness" (Wilde 2002, p. 44).

(In a conversation Wilde had with me while she was working on her dissertation, she wondered how a revolution could have come from the top down. Such collective behavior would not fit in the elegant paradigms that Zald and Berger developed some years ago. I think the answer is that the Vatican Council was a new kind of collective behavior, one in which the top leader undercut the rigid controls his staff tried to impose on the bishops of the world. The control of course has since been restored.)

Many of the bishops attributed the euphoria of the Council to the direct work of the Holy Spirit.[2] An energy, a force, a dynamism outside themselves was driving them forward. They were encountering opposition and experiencing occasional defeats, but they knew the pope was on their side (Pope Paul perhaps less enthusiastically than Pope John). They voted by overwhelming majorities for reform measures about which many of them had never thought before (regarding issues such as a vernacular liturgy, anti-Semitism, and religious freedom, for example) or which they would have opposed before the Council convened. The Holy Spirit was with them.

Having been present at the third session of the Council in 1965,[3] I am convinced that Wilde has caught exactly what was happening—a Durkheimian effervescence permeated the Aula of San Pietro and various residences at night. Was it collective behavior or was it the Holy Spirit? Does one have to choose? Is not the Spirit quite capable of working through collective behavior?

Wilde also shows how the "liberal" leaders of the Council mobilized resources to achieve the ideal of a reformed Church that came with their newfound hope. They worked through the formal institution of the ecumenical secretariat, in the informal institution of twenty influential bishops meeting each week at the Domus Marie center in Rome,[4] and through informal contacts with Protestant and Orthodox observers. These efforts at organization and coordination were in effect a temporary social movement, energized by the original effervescence, to build large majorities for the principal documents of the Council. The Curia, accustomed as it was to rule by sheer authority, was unable to match such organizational effectiveness. Members of the Curia waited and bided their time.

The bishops went home from the Council. Most of them left their effervescence in Rome. Afraid of hostile reactions from the laity, many of them tried to reassure these folks, whom they assumed to be too simpleminded to grasp what had happened at the Council, that nothing much had really changed. However, the euphoria of the Council had, I suggest, spread to many of the lower clergy and the laity.[5] They too were caught up in enthusiasm for the changes, some of which (like the new liturgy) they were already implementing. The changing attitudes of priests on birth control and masturbation described previously (and documented in NORC 1972) demonstrated that the old structures were eroding only a few years after the end of the Council. The euphoria spread via articles in the Catholic and secular press, summer workshops, conversations among priests and between priests and laity. As early as 1965, when the Council was just ending, people were asking in confession about birth control and priests were telling them to follow their own consciences. Three-quarters of priests expected celibacy to become optional within ten years.[6] It was a time when "anything goes"—or better, "everything is going"—seemed to be the order of the day.

I was caught up in this collective behavior, though I didn't realize it until I read Wilde's dissertation. I did not think that everything would change, as some priests did, but I felt like the sleeping giant had awoken and was flexing its muscles and discovering again its genius. I also felt that under the guise of enthusiasm for the Council a lot of false prophets were running about. The confident Church was, as Mr. Dooley would have said, in a "state of chaos."

Did the Second Vatican Council, considered as a historic event, destroy the Church? If the question is rephrased to mean did the Council destroy some of the major structures of the preconciliar Church, the answer must be that it did and that the lower clergy and the laity, caught in a similar state of euphoria as the bishops had felt at the Council, finished the job. Whether that be good or bad or a mixture of good and bad, readers must judge for themselves.

It must be noted, however, that other structures survived, especially the core matters of religious doctrine—a fact overlooked by those who damn the Council. Paradoxically, though the bishops had said little about either subject, the structures concerning sex and authority were the ones that collapsed—perhaps because, as Wilde suggests, the bishops were not permitted to address issues of sexuality.

When the bishops came to Rome, many of them felt that something had to be done about the liturgy and about ecumenism. Many believed that attention should be paid to the role of bishops in relationship to Rome. Americans thought something had to be done about Jews and religious freedom. Some felt that the birth control issue should be addressed, but Pope Paul removed that from discussion. None had any intention of dismantling the structures of authority in the Church. Yet by changing anything, they created the possibility that everything could change. Caught up in the euphoria, the lower clergy and the laity changed many other things. The bursting of the wineskins was therefore a two-part process, both parts of which were carried out in moods of effervescence, one in Rome and one all over the Catholic world. By 1970, the laity and the lower clergy had changed most of the structures of the Church they found objectionable—those regarding birth control, divorce, masturbation, authority, Sunday Mass, and premarital sex (and later, homosexuality and in vitro fertilization). If you had been taught that nothing had ever changed, nothing would change, nothing could change, and then something did, the changers, without intending it, would have put everything in doubt. In a period as short as perhaps five years, there had been a Catholic revolution the likes of which the Church had never seen before. Attempts to undo it have had no success.

One of the reasons for this sudden and dramatic revolution was that the resources available to support the old structures were not very strong. The wineskins were fragile, perhaps leaking already. The principal motivational resources available to the Church were, first, the Church (or the pope) says so and you must obey without question, and second, you will commit mortal sin and go to hell if you don't. When arguments were advanced to support the rules they were usually in an abstract and ecclesiastical language that most laity (and many clergy) could not understand. Thus the philosophical explanations for why every act of married

intercourse must be open to the possibility of creating
however valid, simply made no sense to married laype
1968 birth control encyclical was doubly unfortunate
dismissed the issue without responding to the reasons
commission had given for change. Thus the reaction o
and the lower clergy to the encyclical was caused in p
fact that the wineskins were already bursting, and in its tu
them completely apart.

Blind obedience may have worked with peasants;
work with educated laity. Church leaders made (and ma
rible mistake when they assume that it will or should. (In
chapter I will discuss how the laity disposed of the fear of

Could the American bishops, if they had been more a
more credible as pastors and had possessed better theolo
sources and media skills, have directed the process more
Perhaps, but in the long run, it probably would not ha
much difference. An article in the *Catholic Historian* (19
how, in 1967, Archbishop Paul Hallinan of Atlanta, on
architects of the Constitution on the Sacred Liturgy, st
desperately to establish five centers on university campuse
sponsible liturgical experimentation. The Vatican ha
plained about reports of liturgical innovations that wer
bizarre—Mass with martinis and crackers, for example. H
thought that the answer to uncontrolled liturgical experi
tion was supervised experimentation, not a bad idea in
cumstances. In terrible health, he fought bitterly at a mee
the hierarchy against two staunchly conservative car
Patrick O'Boyle and James Francis McIntyre, for his pr
and, astonishingly, won. Rome rejected the proposal a
American hierarchy lost its influence in liturgical reform. S

attempts to ride the whirlwind would probably have been rejected. On the other hand, they would have been worth trying.

But it is self-deceiving to argue that there is nothing in the actual documents of Vatican II to legitimate the collapse of the old structures. For the documents themselves—those on liturgy, Scripture, religious freedom, the modern world, other faiths (especially Judaism), ecumenism—contributed substantially to the weakening of pre-existing structures.

If "blame" is to be found for the Catholic revolution, it might not be unlike that adduced by Sewell to account for the French Revolution—the Church had waited too long to attempt change. Moreover, it had not realized that it was not teaching illiterate and docile peasants anymore and neglected the task of talking to its laity and lower clergy in a manner they could understand and accept.[7]

Reflecting again on my discussion with the senior prelate, I conclude, after considering the theoretical frameworks provided by Sewell and Wilde, that after the interventions by Frings and Lienart and their acceptance by John XXIII, there was no way to prevent Vatican II from becoming a revolutionary event. Sociology, to repeat, has no means of measuring whether what the cardinals proposed was wise as well as well-intentioned, or whether the consequences are, in the main, to be welcomed or condemned.

To put the issue bluntly for those who demand a return to the "old days," either immediately or more gradually and subtly, let's assume an extreme case: Put the Mass back in Latin and reverse the altars again (as Cardinal Ratzinger wants), reject religious freedom, call Protestants heretics and schismatics again, restore the title "perfidious" to the Jews, ban current scriptural research and return to the rulings of the Modernist controversy, restore

the Index of Forbidden Books, write into law that which is in practice the case—that bishops are only functionaries working for the Roman Curia—and issue a denunciation of the modern world like the Syllabus of Errors from the nineteenth century. What will happen? Much harm will be done to the Church.

Yet you will have not restored the Catholic world of the late 1950s, not in the slightest. The shredded wineskins cannot be repaired. To blame Pope John and the Vatican Council is to refuse to face the critical question of why the old structures—the patterns and their supporting motivations—collapsed so easily and so quickly.

My colleague and friend Mark Chaves has argued that secularization should be conceptualized as a decline in religious authority and not as a decline in religious faith or practice (Chaves 1994). The decline in authority of religious institutions, he suggests, is the result of social differentiation in which many new institutions have their own share of authority. It is a useful distinction. Political parties and activist groups have gained authority in controlling voting behavior, and churches have less control in the political world than they once did. Perhaps this institutional differentiation provided some of the context for the Catholic revolution. But in itself the theory does not explain why the changes in the Church were so abrupt and so comprehensive. However, Chaves's theory suggests that there may be long-term strains in society, which makes it unlikely that religious authority lost can easily be regained.

Is Catholic revolution too strong a metaphor? A case can be made that it was not really a revolution. There was no destruction of top-level leadership. All denominations went through changes in the second half of the twentieth century. Perhaps the changes would have come anyway. Lienart and Frings did not intend to start a revolution, just to make some modest changes and to weaken the power of the Curia to block such changes.

The metaphor is debatable, as are all metaphors. If anyone can come up with a better one I would be delighted to hear it. I would argue, however, that the key element in the Catholic revolution was the demolition of the structure that said that the Catholic Church would not, could not ever change. This demolition was accomplished by the pope and the Council fathers against the mid-level authority in the Church (which perhaps makes it a revolution, a collective behavior, sui generis). In the immediate post-conciliar years, the lower clergy and the laity overturned the power of the Papacy to demand obedience on a selected range of issues. It was a nuanced revolution in which other patterns and motivations were preserved—because, as we shall see subsequently, the lower clergy and the laity liked them.

Moreover, the speed of the change that took place in patterns that had persisted for hundreds and in some cases a thousand years or more was certainly revolutionary. Other denominations changed too, but not quite so rapidly or systematically. Would the same rapid changes have occurred if Lienart and Frings had not protested on the first day of the first session and if the organizers at the Domus Marie had not been so sophisticated and effective? Given the history of Catholicism in the years before the Council, it seems unlikely that in the absence of some kind of dramatic, overturning event—not unlike the Council itself—the changes would have come so quickly, so systematically, or so efficiently.

A nuanced revolution, a revolution sui generis indeed, but, in the absence of a better metaphor, still a revolution.

SIX

How Do They Stay?

Granted that in the Catholic revolution of the late 1960s the lower clergy and the laity in effect repealed many of the rules they did not understand or like, how can priests and laity reject an essential, or allegedly essential, dimension of the Church's teaching and still act as though they were devout, churchgoing Catholics?

Before 1965 the model was clear and precise: If you were a Catholic (in this country at any rate), you accepted what the Church said on everything, large or small, important or unimportant. When Rome decided a difficult matter, your choice was simple. Either you went along, perhaps reluctantly, and stayed in the Church, or you dissented and, again perhaps reluctantly, decamped from the Church.

This model was so hallowed and so unquestioned that its violation still affronts right-wing Catholics and departed Catholics and secular journalists who wonder how you can have a Catholic Church when many Catholics insist that they will affiliate on their terms and not the Church's terms. (Let us leave aside, for the purpose of this discussion, the fact that canon law assumes you stop being a Catholic only when you formally renounce your religion.)

Obviously the model has changed, but unless we understand the religious dynamics of the change, we will misunderstand what is perhaps the most important development in recent American Catholic history. In this chapter I propose to search for understanding using data from a 1979 study of Catholics under the age of thirty (Fee et al. 1981) and my own theory of the religious imagination (Greeley 1995). The answer to the question How do they get away with it? is simple, though the sociological path to the answer is somewhat intricate.

Briefly, my theory, based upon the work of Weber, Parsons, Geertz, James, and Otto, contends that religion is originally and primarily behavior that occurs in that dimension of the human personality variously called the preconscious, the poetic faculty, the creative imagination, or even (if one is an Aristotelian) the agent intellect.

Religion takes its origin in experiences that renew hope (phenomena that might be called "grace experiences"). These hope-renewing experiences leave residues in the imagination that have, to quote Geertz, unique and special characteristics because they provide explanations for the meaning and purpose of human life and hence can be called symbols, and the experiences and symbols (usually, if not always, correlating with the overriding symbols of one's religious heritage) are shared with others through narratives or stories. Social action is value oriented; religious values are the ultimate values of one's life and are contained in symbol, repeated in stories, and based on experiences that renew hope and give (usually preconscious) meaning and purpose to one's life.

Facing the problem of the church attendance of dissident

Catholics from such a theoretical perspective, I was led to expect that dissident Catholics would continue to attend church regularly if their religious experiences and their religious images served to cancel out any dissonance that might exist between their ethical convictions and frequent church services.

Ideally, one would have looked at that proportion of the Catholic population—approximately 85 percent—that rejects the Church's birth control teachings. Unfortunately, data on the religious imagination are contained only in the 1979 NORC study of American and Canadian Catholics between the ages of eighteen and thirty (Fee et al. 1981). In this population group, more than 90 percent rejected the Church's birth control ethic. There were not enough non-dissident respondents to make analysis of this variable possible. Instead, a question about couples living together before marriage was chosen. Twenty-three percent of the young Catholic adults thought that such behavior was always wrong or almost always wrong, while 77 percent thought it was wrong sometimes or never. The proportion of these two groups that attended church regularly (at least two or three times a month) differed sharply. Fifty-eight percent of those who disapproved of premarital cohabitation attended church regularly, as opposed to only 28 percent of the dissidents.

The problem is not so much the different rates of church attendance, but rather why some 28 percent of those who seemed to flatly reject the sexual teaching of the Church are still regular churchgoers. A hypothesis, derived from the religious imagination theory summarized above, would suggest that a positive image of God might account for the ability of the dissidents to harmonize their dissidence with Church teaching and regular attendance. Experiencing themselves as close to God and being likely to think of God as a "lover," I hypothesized, might cancel out any inconsistency between doctrinal and devotional practices.

There are two different ways that religious imagination variables might function. There might be an "intervening" variable between ethical dissent and church attendance, or there might be an interacting variable exercising influence on church attendance only for dissidents.

In the first case, because the dissidents are less likely to think of God as a "lover" and because they are less likely to think of themselves as close to God, they are less likely to go to church. Such an explanation copes with the question of how dissidents can attend church regularly by eliminating the problem. Dissidence, as such, does not affect church attendance, save indirectly—in this case, because the dissidents do not have such positive religious imaginations. There is a certain amount of improbability in such an explanation, for it seems to eliminate all conflict between an ethical stand on the one hand and devotional behavior on the other. It seems improbable that in the real world there was less tension between the two aspects of Catholic affiliation in 1979.

In the second possible explanation, there would be no correlation or very little correlation between the strength of the religious imagination and church attendance for those who are not dissident and a moderate to strong correlation between the imagination and behavior of the dissident. In such a case, there would be no difference in church attendance between dissidents and non-dissidents whose closeness to God and perception of God as a "lover" were high; but as the intensity of the religious imagination diminishes, the rates of church attendance will diminish sharply for the dissidents and slightly or not at all for the non-dissidents.

Such a possibility seems inherently more attractive, as it suggests that the religious imagination cancels out the church attendance effect of the dissent for those who have a strong religious imagination. The latter is a countervailing force acting against the effect of ethical dissent when dissent is present and having no impact, because an effect is not required, among those who do not dissent.

Closeness to God, in this research, was measured by asking the respondent to place himself somewhere in a series of five concentric circles that depicted closeness to God; and the image of God as a "lover" was part of a series of items that the respondents were asked to rank according to their reaction to them (some of the other images were of God as "creator," "judge," "master," "father," "redeemer," and "mother"). These two items were chosen because one seemed to be a satisfactory indicator of religious experience and the other a satisfactory indicator of religious imagery and because it was hypothesized that those who felt close to God and pictured God as a "lover" would be likelier than others to think that God would be tolerant of dissent from Church teachings. While God might not necessarily approve of dissidence, God might be presumed to be rather more pleased with the dissident's being in church regularly than with his not being there. Those who are "lovers" normally want to have their beloved around.

Some 30 percent of the respondents were "extremely likely" to picture God as a "lover" and 19 percent placed themselves in the bull's-eye of the circle, "very close" to God. What was the nature of the relationship between these two aspects of the religious imagination and church attendance? And was this relationship different for the dissidents and the non-dissidents? Correlation coefficients presented established that the anticipated interaction does, indeed, occur. For the dissidents, the correlation between regular church attendance and a sense of closeness to God was .32, whereas for non-dissidents, the relationship is zero. For the former, the correlation between the image of God as "lover" and church attendance was a significant .19 and for the latter, a statistically insignificant .08. The religious imagination, in other words, had no effect on church attendance for those who accepted the Church's sexual ethic, and a considerable influence on church attendance for those who did not accept the sexual ethic.

Do these correlation coefficients "account" for the different levels of church attendance and thus adequately explain why some dissident Catholics still show up at Mass on Sunday morning (or on Saturday evening)? As the results of multiple regression show, the first interaction (experience of God) accounted for half the difference, and the second interaction (image of God) accounted for the other half. Quite simply, some Catholics who dissent are able to attend church regularly because the intensity of their religious imagination experience and imagery cancels out the negative impact of their ethical dissent, and one need not search any further for an explanation.

Young Catholics who had a strong feeling of closeness to God, were extremely likely to imagine God as a "lover," and who also rejected the Church's sexual teaching were as likely to attend church regularly as their counterparts on the religious imagination measures. Dissidents were less likely than non-dissidents to go to church regularly only at the low end of the religious imagination scale. Strong imagery of God kept young Catholics close to their Church even when ethical dissent might otherwise have led them to lower levels of religious devotion. In the absence of such strong imagery, dissidence did indeed lead to less intense religious devotion.

It does not seem likely that Church leadership will succeed in changing this behavior simply by insisting on the power of its own authority. Dissidents were significantly less likely than non-dissidents to think that the pope is infallible and to endorse the primacy of authority of Peter and his successors (20 percent versus 34 percent). It is interesting to note that the overwhelming majority of even the non-dissidents did not strongly endorse these Catholic doctrines, which have received so much emphasis in the last century.

There were no significant differences between the two groups in the frequency of the reception of Holy Communion and activity in parish organizations and reflection on the purpose of life and the experience of God. More than one-third of those who rejected the Church's teaching on premarital sex received Holy Communion as often as they attended church. Their ability to cope with religious strain was manifested not only in their church attendance, but also in their reception of the Eucharist. However, these dissidents were neither malcontents nor anticlerical. They did not differ from the non-dissidents who attended church regularly in their approval of the quality of preaching, the empathy of their parish priest, and their approval of the way the pope, the bishop, and the pastor performed their jobs. Moreover, they were not significantly less likely to approve the possibility of their daughter's becoming a nun. Finally, there were no significant differences in the proportions of those who had favorable attitudes toward the Church, who felt moderately close to the Church, who talked about religious problems with a priest, who had recently read spiritual books, or who had served as lay lectors or ministers at Mass.

The dissidents were, however, likelier to have had serious doubts about their faith and, if they had had doubts, were also likelier to have resolved them. Religious dissidents who attended church regularly seemed to be young men and women who had serious questions about their religion and resolved these questions in favor of a God of intimacy and love and against an institutional Church that sought to impose ethical norms on them.

Were such young men and women hedonists and materialists and captives of the "contraceptive mentality," a phrase that continues to be found in recent hierarchical warnings? In fact, dissidents and non-dissidents did not differ in their thinking about the ideal age of marriage or the ideal number of children (at least three). How could anyone say that young people who thought that the ideal was to have at least three children were victims of a "contraceptive mentality"? Nor is there a significant difference between the two groups in their conviction that the first pregnancy after marriage should come within two years.

The 1979 study provides a picture of Catholics born after 1949 and before 1964, the first generation to grow into young adulthood after the Council. An understanding of how they coped with the revolutionary situation in which they found themselves illustrates the dynamics at work in those years. Catholics were rejecting the old rules but not rejecting the Church or God. Rather, they were shifting their appeal from a Church that did not understand to a God that did.

I am not defending the "cafeteria Catholics" of 1979 or subsequent years. I am instead trying to understand their religious posture. I am not saying that dissidents love God more; I am saying that those dissidents whose experience and images of God are intimate do not stay away from church. Nor am I saying that those who have intense relationships with God are likelier to be dissident. Rather, I am saying that men and women with intense relationships are not kept away from church (where God is) by dissent from sexual teachings.

There are two major and glacial shifts that the data seem to indicate, first, a shift away from appeals to institutional Church leadership and toward appeals to God, and second, a conviction that God does not want you to stay away from church because you reject a specific teaching of the Church. The devout dissidents are rejecting any claim by the leadership to have a monopoly on God. The dynamics that make selective Catholicism possible seem to be impervious to the influence of the magisterium.

Did not these young people, who probably are like their parents and now their children in their decisions about how to be Catholics on their own terms, in effect become just like Protestants in their choice of individual interpretation over hierarchal authority? One can make the case that they did not. Even in the traditional Catholic moral theology the ultimate norm for moral behavior is the choice of the individual conscience. Moral theologians before the Council argued that the conscience had to be informed by the teaching of the Church. Either that teaching is the sole determinant of the choice or there is room for other influences—such as the conviction that in particular cases the Church authority does not really understand the problem.

If the former is the case, then the decision of the moral actor is like that of an automaton: good Catholics do what they are told and that is that. If the latter is the case, if one dissents in good faith, then one does not leave the household of the faith. In the years since the Council, large numbers of Catholics have dissented (generally on matters of sex and authority only) and have not left the household of the faith. As to their good faith, that is a matter beyond sociological judgment and is perhaps best left to God.

Large numbers of Catholics in the years since the Council have been able to rationalize the apparent conflict between their Catholic allegiance and their dissent from Catholic sexual teaching. The question that remains is why they would want to bother. Why not simply leave the Church?

SEVEN

New Rules, New Prophets, and Beige Catholicism

Revolutionary events and the collapse of institutional structures (paradigms and their motivations) always leave chaos, confusion, and conflict in their wake.[1] The conflicts over the French Revolution, energized by the storming of the Bastille as its eventful symbol, continued in France until the return of Charles de Gaulle from Colombey in 1958. A fervent Catholic and a fervent Republican, *le général* provided the occasion for healing the breach between the Church and the Republic, an occasion many on both sides had sought for years. The shape of the Fifth Republic seems to have institutionalized that new tolerance. Will the confusion within Catholicism continue for another two centuries?

Probably not. Those who dissent from the Council and from the subsequent collapse of the rules have been revitalized by the pontificate of John Paul II, but they are only a small minority (e.g., only about 12 percent of the U.S. population agrees with the Church's stance on birth control), and there is no reason to think their numbers will increase. Nonetheless, in the three decades since the effervescence of the Council dissipated, the chaos in the Church has continued unabated. The leadership continues its authoritarian rule making. The majority of the laity and the lower clergy do not obey. The leadership cannot and will not accept that making rules is no longer effective; the laity and the lower clergy will not accept the dicta of a leadership that does not listen.

In the revolutionary years immediately after the Council, more changed than just the rules about sex. While the large majority of laity and lower clergy participated in and celebrated these changes, other groups were busily engaged in destroying or trying to destroy other elements of Catholicism that they did not like. Much of the ceremony and art of the Catholic tradition was summarily rejected, without vote or even consultation. The altars were stripped, to use the phrasing in the title of Eamon Duffy's book on the Reformation in England. The leaders of this secondary revolution banned statues, stained glass windows, votive candles, crucifixes, and representational art from new or remodeled churches. They rejected popular devotions like May crownings, processions, First Communions, incense, classical polyphony, and Gregorian chant. They dismissed the rosary, angels, saints, the souls in purgatory, and Mary the mother of Jesus. They considered these old customs and devotions liturgically or ecumenically or politically incorrect.

There was nothing in any of the documents of the Council to justify the stripping of the altars. The Council never said, never even hinted that Catholic churches should be made to look like Protestant churches or Quaker meeting halls. The Council did not argue that guitars were superior to organs, or folk songs to traditional hymns. It certainly did not proclaim that devotion to the Mother of Jesus was no longer appropriate. However, the post-revolutionary chaos in the Church made it easy for some of those in various powerful movements—ecumenical, liturgical, educational, and, later, feminist—to take control of the direction of change in their own areas of concern and impose their views on many parishes, usually without consulting the membership. The ordinary lay folk were objects to be transformed and not citizens whose rights merited respect.

Professor Duffy has noted that few if any theologians have reflected on Mary the Mother of Jesus since the Council. However, Garry Wills and Elizabeth Johnson have advocated the abandonment of devotion to her, Wills on the grounds that Pope John Paul II is dedicated to that devotion and Johnson because it is "patriarchal" (Wills 2000, Johnson 2000). (Johnson is one of those hard feminists who think that the use of that label is enough to settle a debate.) Thus is the most powerful religious symbol of the last millennium and a half stripped from the altar.

These various movements subverted much of the richness of the Catholic imaginative and communal tradition in the name of being "correct" and "postconciliar." There was nothing to be learned from the preconciliar past, from anything that had happened before 1965. It is surprising that few voices were raised against this stripping of the altars. It is even more surprising that the Catholic bishops in this country issued a document that seemed to imply that the proper Catholic parish church should look pretty much like a Benedictine monastery. No one seemed to understand that they were destroying precisely that sacramental dimension of the Catholic heritage that was more important than prosaic rules and that held Catholics in their Church regardless of what else happened.

In principle it should have been possible to reform the Church in line with the conciliar documents and not replace the Catholic imaginative heritage with cold and cliché-ridden textbooks. However, neither historical nor theological nor personal depth was a resource available in abundance in the immediate post-revolutionary era. The result was what theologian Robert Barron calls "beige Catholicism," the colorless, odorless, tasteless, unimaginative, unpoetic variety of Catholicism in which he was raised (Barron 2000). The baby had been thrown out with the bathwater—and the baby's mother, too.

Moreover, many on the lower levels of Church leadership—especially in the parishes—still felt the need for order and certainty. Priests and nuns, once blessed, as they thought, with the charism of knowing the answers, all the answers, searched desperately for new sources of certainty. Out of this search, new "experts" appeared—men and women who again knew all the answers (though their answers shifted over the years). A summer week of sessions on the "new" Bible studies made some instant experts on the Scriptures. A master's degree in counseling and guidance made others do-it-yourself psychoanalysts. Annual liturgical meetings kept yet others up-to-date on the latest liturgical fashions. A master's degree in pastoral theology made some instant theologians. A weekend worship provided all the tips one needed for religious education. A quote, not infrequently out of context, from a celebrity theologian (Küng, Rahner, Schillebeeckx—though not Lonergan or Tracy, who, being Americans, didn't count) was sufficient to settle an argument.

These ill-trained and frequently emotionally immature prophets spread across the land, clinging desperately to their usually small fragment of truth as though it were the whole truth and hassling the laity to change with the times and enthusiastically adopt postconciliar Catholicism.

As best we can trace the attitudes of the laity during those years, they displayed amazing tolerance toward the false prophets. They may have disliked the arbitrary dictates of the parish liturgist or the parish director of religious education, but they generally regarded them as annoyances that had to be tolerated because they still liked being Catholic and because they were pleased with the more sensible structures that were emerging in the Church, whether officially approved or not. Media surveys repeatedly demonstrated that relatively few Catholics had left the Church and that a large majority thought they could be good Catholics on their own terms, liked the effects of the Council, and were not about to leave the Church. Moreover, belief in core doctrines like Jesus and the Sacraments and life after death were not affected by the postconciliar changes. In fact, belief in life after death had increased since the Council (Greeley and Hout 1999).

The next phase was the emergence of "renewal" movements, which strove to remodel the lay folk, so to speak. These various interventions—charismatic groups, cursillos, encounter groups, parish renewal groups, sensitivity training, Rite of Christian Initiation of Adults (RCIA) groups—heavily emphasized the psychological, if not to say psychological manipulation, and were little concerned with substance or with the religious needs of the people who participated. The thinking was that one did not need to know about these needs because they were probably false consciousness anyway, and because the goal of the experience was to "reform" the participants. A less pleasant word might be "brainwash."

In the hands of skilled, flexible, and mature leaders, all of these interventions can achieve modest success and leave the personalities of the participants undamaged.[2] However, often these various interventions involved high-pressure, emotionally charged weekends deliberately designed to temporarily unhinge the participants so that they could be remade in the image and likeness of the people administering the intervention. No psychologically sophisticated person expects that a weekend of such experiences will permanently affect the habits and the behavior of those who are forced to submit to it. Humans are far more durable than that. You may be able to take them apart temporarily and brutalize them emotionally. They will, however, recover in due course.

Often those in charge of such interludes are true believers (read "false prophets") who are determined that the participants will come out of the experience as remodeled Catholics, true believers like themselves. It usually doesn't work that way. One can always explain the failure as the result of obdurate false consciousness.

The RCIA process is not a weekend event but a year-long (or even longer) replacement for the old "convert classes." It is based on an aprioristic guide for the initiation of adults. Rarely does it consider the place where the participants are in their way to the Church or whether those who are already baptized should be put through the process. The RCIA director has considerable power, including the power to deny that one is worthy of baptism, that one can consider oneself a member of the chosen.

The process is dense in anachronisms—the "catechumens" are dismissed from Mass after the homily, following the practice of the ancient Church, which feared that agents of the Roman Empire might slip in and spy on the sacred rites. In fact, the Roman

Empire has not been around for a long time. "Scrutinies" determine whether a person is worthy of baptism. "Mystagogy" imparts the great secrets of Catholic faith to the catechumens. Despite the endless possibility of manipulations and the goofy language and the lack of substantive content, RCIA is sometimes very successful, though only if the director is secure personally and not an ideologue. In those cases it can be a great boon for parish priests, who no longer have to worry about convert classes. Unfortunately, as many parish priests and bishops will admit off the record, even those RCIA directors who are flexible and mature rarely have adequate training for the role.

In all of these rites and experiences, one detects little concern for the rights or dignity of the participants. The impulse to transform them and the perennial temptation to do good, to manufacture, indeed to mass produce, virtue is often irresistible. In addition, in a time of chaos and confusion, Catholic clergy and the quasi clergy who serve as replacements for the younger curates who are no more tend to fall victim to authoritarian pragmatism and the theory that if you force people to be good and to do good things, they will eventually develop habits of virtue. Aquinas taught that virtue resulted from a frequent replication of free acts. In busy postconciliar parish life, there's just no time for free acts, so one has to be content with repetition.

Although priests no longer control the lives (especially the sex lives) of the laity, priests and parish staff members do still control access to the Sacraments, though canon law explicitly denies them the right to refuse the Sacraments save in extraordinary circumstances. Unfortunately canon law rarely vindicates this right, because the laypeople are unaware of it.

So, while in the post-revolutionary years after 1970, when the old rules were collapsing, a new set of extra canonical rules came into existence, rules that protected clerical power and abused the rights of the laity. Paradoxically, the new freedom also meant new and harsh rules. The rule-making power of the local clergy proved remarkably durable.

These were bad times. The winds of change Pope John had let in when he opened his window of *aggiornamento* were howling like a hurricane. Small wonder that some of those who had made the Council, like Joseph Ratzinger, turned against it. They may have talked revolution, a word that was popular in the late 1960s and early 1970s, but when it happened to their Church and in the real (structure destroying) sense of the word, they tried, and are still trying, to play the Thermidorian game of restoration. They did not comprehend, any more than most of the Council fathers or the leaders of the Church, that change had been postponed for so long that even very moderate changes would cause a revolutionary collapse. They saw their lives approaching an end in a context of a disintegrating Church and did not have the nerve or the faith to accept the bursting of the wineskins, for which they themselves were responsible. They blamed the Council because they couldn't blame themselves. In the meantime, at the grass-roots level authoritarian pragmatism was doing constant violence to the ordinary laity, a situation of which the local chanceries and the Vatican were serenely unaware.

The new authoritarians make the old monsignors look permissive. In the pre–Vatican II Church, the authoritarian pragmatists had broad control over the lives of the laity. Now their control is limited to impeding access to the Sacraments. With the exception of some pre-Cana sessions—by no means all—I have never heard a good word about any of the sacramental preparations. "Boring!" is the usual description of them. Still, it makes us priests feel good to process people through them because afterward we can tell ourselves that now they at least know what they ought to believe and how they ought to behave. Many of these sessions, I'm told, are little more than discussion groups about Biblical passages that have nothing to do with the Sacrament the people forced into the group want to receive.

The Church is now busy prating about the most recent buzzword, "evangelization," which ought to mean preaching the good news. Maybe in some places this really is a celebration of the joy and beauty of the Gospel. In most cases of which I have heard, it is the same old thing, a barely disguised authoritarian pragmatism, devoid of beauty. We even claim that we are evangelizing the "un-Churched," as if anyone would be attracted to a religious group that is still all rules and no beauty.

In revolutionary times, not all movement among the masses is in one direction. Forces and counterforces struggle. New ideas are discovered just as old ones are being discarded. New leaders emerge as old leaders disappear. Old rules are abolished, to be replaced by new rules. No one is in charge, at least not for very long. Anything goes and everything goes. The heavy hand of the old Church is replaced by an unappealing beige Catholicism. The blind lead the blind. Confusion is made worse by more (and unnecessary) confusion.

Why do Catholics put up with all this stuff (not to use more scatological language)? Rome continues to harass them about sex and the local parish denies the Sacraments to them and their children. Why bother?

The answer is that they like being Catholic and they want the Catholic Sacraments for themselves and for their children.

EIGHT

Only in America?

Might not this revolution that I have described have been a uniquely American phenomenon? Curial bureaucrats (particularly Dr. Navarro-Vals, the pope's press spokesman) delight in saying that American problems are unique and are the result of the materialism, consumerism, secularism, and "pan-sexualism" of American society. The curialists, however, are European or European-influenced intellectuals, which means that they are obdurate haters of the United States. Thus, at the time of the worst period of the child sex abuse scandals, the curialists took the position that this was what one might expect in a country where everyone was obsessed with sex, and that the American hierarchy had been frightened into its Dallas charter for the protection of children by pressure from the media. One might wonder where the countries are in which people are not obsessed with sex. Moreover, there is substantial evidence that child abuse is part of the human condition and that it's a problem in the priesthood everywhere. The Church in the United States is merely ahead of the Church in other countries in its attempts to cope with sexual abuse by priests.

By the same logic, curialists and conservative Catholics might well contend that the revolution among the laity and the lower clergy after the Council was a uniquely American phenomenon—interesting, perhaps, but of no great importance for the universal Church. The data reported in this book would therefore have no application to other countries. An alternative explanation is that the United States was ahead of other countries in collecting data with which to chart the bursting wineskins. Is there any evidence that Americans are in fact likelier to have been influenced by revolution than Catholics in other countries?

There are, alas, no good international data from the 1960s or the early 1970s to replicate the American pattern. However, data collected by the International Social Survey Program in 1998 enable one to judge whether American Catholics are any more sex-mad than Catholics in other countries, and a seven-nation study of attitudes toward the next papal election carried out by Michael Hout and myself in 1998 makes it possible to say whether American Catholics are more dissatisfied with the organizational structures of the Church than Catholics in other countries.

Table 5 presents the attitudes of Catholics in twenty-two countries surveyed by the International Social Survey Program on the issues of premarital sex, homosexual sex, and legalized abortion in cases of poverty.

Twenty percent of American Catholics thought that premarital sex was always wrong. Only three countries had significantly higher scores, the Philippines (63 percent), Chile (30 percent), and Brazil (42 percent). The American proportion is slightly higher than Spain (18 percent), Poland (19 percent), and Italy (19 percent).

Table 5. *Sexual Attitudes of Catholics in Twenty-Two Countries, 1998*

	Premarital sex always wrong	Homosexual sex always wrong	Abortion always wrong, even for the poor
Australia (306)	23%	54%	38%
West Germany (379)	6%	29%	43%
Britain (69)	14%	41%	49%
United States (343)	20%	55%	54%
Austria (805)	2%	35%	34%
Hungary (545)	21%	69%	13%
Italy (886)	19%	59%	46%
Ireland (842)	21%	62%	41%
Netherlands (392)	19%	14%	37%
Czech Republic (562)	5%	40%	25%
Slovenia (712)	3%	54%	20%
Poland (1,053)	19%	76%	46%
Canada (236)	9%	36%	40%
Philippines (1,026)	63%	84%	71%
Spain (2,057)	18%	37%	40%
Latvia (243)	12%	65%	31%
Slovakia (885)	19%	61%	31%
France (548)	8%	53%	18%
Portugal (1,072)	24%	78%	46%
Switzerland (578)	5%	31%	30%
Chile (1,108)	30%	88%	76%
Brazil (1,585)	42%	83%	88%

SOURCE: International Social Survey Program, 1998.

NOTE: The number of Catholics interviewed in each country is in parentheses after the name of the country. The numbers vary greatly depending on the size of the original sample and the proportion of the population that is Catholic.

Sex crazy, huh?

Fifty-five percent of American Catholics thought that homosexual sex was always wrong, as compared to 37 percent of Spaniards, 59 percent of Italians, and 76 percent of Poles. American Catholics were likelier to think that such sex was always wrong than West Germans, Britons, Austrians, Netherlanders, Canadians, Czechs, and the French (albeit in the last case only slightly).

Thus the propensity of the curialists to attribute the sex abuse scandal to the greater tolerance of Americans for homosexuality seems to be based on a priori conviction, rather than on any evidence.

Finally, American Catholics were likelier to think that abortion was morally wrong even in a poor family (54 percent) than anyone except Filipinos (71 percent), Chileans (76 percent), and Brazilians (88 percent). Thus they were more disapproving of abortion than Catholics in Poland (46 percent), Spain (40 percent), and Italy (46 percent), among other countries.

It is time for the Vatican to declare a moratorium on scapegoating the allegedly sex crazy American culture. There is no evidence in table 5 to sustain the argument that a revolution against the Church's sexual rules occurred only in the United Sates.

In 1998 Michael Hout and I, with the help of a number of our International Social Survey Program colleagues, endeavored to develop a job description for the next pope. We developed a questionnaire that was administered in seven countries (the United States, Ireland, Poland, Spain, Italy, West Germany, and the Philippines). The questionnaire began with an introductory paragraph that read, "We are interested in what type of leader Catholics would like to see elected the next pope. As you may know, when a pope dies the cardinals meet in Rome to elect the next pope. The last time a pope was elected was in 1978 when Pope John Paul II was elected."

We followed this preamble with seven questions (more in some countries) that addressed concerns with the institutional form of the Catholic Church. If Americans were likelier to support major institutional change than Catholics in the other six countries, it could be taken as evidence that the ferment after the Council was unique to the United States or at least disproportionate in the United States.

We did not ask about doctrinal issues, save arguably the ordination of women, or matters of faith. Table 6 shows the exact wording of each question and the responses in each country.[1] In every country, a majority of the laity supported change of some sort, and in some countries, majorities supported reform in all seven of the areas of concern.

The most reform-minded countries were Spain and Ireland. These two very Catholic countries wanted change more than any of the others. Each of the seven reforms got support from over 58 percent of Catholics in Spain and Ireland (the exact profile of support differed slightly between them). They were among the countries where the largest majorities stressed a desire that the next pope be more open to change. Spanish Catholics gave particularly strong support to the proposition that the pope should attend more to the life of the laity and grant local bishops more autonomy; they were less keen about the election of local bishops. Irish Catholics particularly favored lay advisers and married priests. Support for the ordination of women was highest in these two countries and Germany (with the United States not far behind).

The United States and Italy fell in the middle of the countries in the study. American Catholics endorsed reform in six of the seven areas by roughly a two-to-one margin. The exception was the question of autonomy for local bishops, which got "only" 58 percent support. The Italians were among the most populist nations, with 77 percent supporting a pope who would emphasize the life of the laity over religious themes. On the other hand, autonomy for local bishops failed (by two percentage points) to get majority support. The Italians also showed a lower level of support for a pope open to change than would be expected given their support for specific changes.

By contrast, Polish Catholics supported specific reforms less than might be expected given their strong (56 percent) support for a pope more open to change. A narrow majority of Poles supported the election of bishops, more autonomy for local bishops, and an emphasis on the life of the laity. The call for lay advisers fell two percentage points short of a majority. Only ordination of women was strongly opposed—but that by a three-to-one margin.

Catholics in the Philippines were the most conservative. A strong majority thought that lay advisers would improve the Church and a slim majority supported electing bishops. None of the other reforms secured the support of the majority. Changes in the composition of the priesthood got particularly strong opposition in the Philippines; Filipinos would prefer to stay with a celibate, male-only clergy by a four-to-one margin.

Remarkably, the only reform to win a majority of support in all seven countries was the election of bishops. Remarkable because this issue is not an item on any group's agenda for change. Many respondents were probably stating an opinion on the matter for the first time when they answered this question (which was not the case with some of the other issues, like the ordination of

Table 6. *Attitudes toward Role of Next Pope, by Country*

	Germany	Spain	Ireland	United States	Italy	Poland	Philippines
Pope should show more concern for life of laity	79%	87%	75%	69%	77%	51%	47%
Pope should allow priests to marry	83%	79%	82%	69%	67%	50%	21%
Bishops should be elected by those in the diocese	75%	58%	63%	65%	67%	55%	51%
Laity should be allowed to advise pope	81%	77%	82%	65%	62%	49%	68%
Local bishops should have more autonomy	75%	74%	63%	58%	48%	53%	37%
Pope should allow women to become priests	71%	71%	67%	65%	58%	24%	18%
Pope should be more open to change	76%	74%	79%	65%	51%	56%	48%
Average[a]	78%	74%	73%	65%	61%	48%	41%
N[b]	422	1080	489	770	687	830	1029

NOTE: Non-respondents are excluded from the base. Data for Germany provided by GiF-Getas; for Spain, by Analysis Sociológicos, Económicos, y Políticos S.A.; for Ireland, by MRBI; for the United States, by Gallup; for Italy, by Eurisko; for Poland, by Demoskop; for the Philippines, by Social Weather Stations.

The questions in the survey were as follows:

1. Which would you consider more important in choosing a pope, that the pope show more concern about what life is like for ordinary people or that the pope should show more concern about religious issues?

2. Would you favor or oppose the next pope permitting priests to marry?

3. Currently Catholic bishops are appointed by the Vatican. In the past bishops were elected by priests and people within their own diocese. Would you prefer the next pope to continue to appoint bishops, or would you prefer to have bishops chosen by priests and people within their own diocese?

4. How would you feel about letting representative laypeople have more of a voice in the Catholic Church, for example by serving as advisers to the pope? Would you favor this?

5. Would you like to see the next pope give more decision making power to the bishops in this country, or do you think the pope should continue to make most of the decisions for the Church?

6. Would you favor or oppose the next pope allowing the ordination of women to the priesthood?

7. Would you like the next pope to be more open to change in the Church, or do you think things are OK the way they are?

[a]Average of responses to all seven questions.

[b]Average of number of non-missing cases across all items.

women and allowing priests to marry, which are widely discussed). They answered in a manner consistent with the democratic institutions that surround them. Each of the seven countries selects its head of government and local officials democratically. When asked about selecting a Church leader democratically, the residents of these countries responded in the affirmative.

No case can or should be made from this papal job description study that these reforms—which would perhaps represent a reform of the Papacy, something that did not happen after the Council—are matters of urgent concern for most lay Catholics in the countries in question. Nor is there any reason to think there would be major defections from the Church in the absence of such reforms. However, the data do fail to make any case that the desire for institutional reform is disproportionate in the United States in comparison with other Catholic countries. Thus, if this desire for reform is a legitimate surrogate measure of the effects of the post-Council revolution (and who would argue that these feelings were widespread in the early 1960s!), then the revolution was not especially powerful in the United States.

The purpose of this chapter was to ascertain whether there is evidence in the international data available to us that Catholic unrest in the United States since 1970 has been excessive in comparison with that in other major Catholic countries. Data both about the Church's sexual ethic and the lay concern for institutional reform fail to sustain such an expectation. Those who want to limit the effects of the revolution to the United States will have to find other sources to support their interpretation.

NINE

Why They Stay

"If you don't like the Catholic Church," the woman in the *Donahue* audience, by her own admission not Catholic, screamed at me, "why don't you stop being a priest and leave the Church?"[1]

I had been criticizing what I took to be the insensitivity of some Catholic leaders to the importance of sex for healing the frictions and wounds of married life and perhaps renewing married love. I was taken aback by the intensity of her anger. Why did it matter so much to her that I had offered some relatively mild criticism? Why did such criticism seem to her to demand that I decamp from Catholicism and the priesthood?

I encounter such anger frequently: if the Church is not perfect, if I disagree with some of the things it does, why don't I get out? I can never quite figure out why the demand is made that the Church alone, of all institutions, must be perfect in order for one to remain attached to it. Perhaps such people want to apply to Catholics the same standard that a certain kind of reactionary Catholicism wishes to apply: you accept everything the pope says or you are not a good Catholic and should leave. You don't like the way the Church treats women? Then leave the Church, don't remain inside and strive for reform. Yet if one were to withdraw from every institution that is unfair to women, one would have to retreat to a desert island.

Find a perfect church and join it, only realize that then it won't be perfect.

But the question persists. In its most naked form it demands to know, "How can someone who is intelligent and well educated continue to be a Roman Catholic in these times?" The question is not a new one. It has been asked by anti-Catholic nativists for 150 years. Often the latent subtext is "How can anyone who is intelligent and well educated believe in any religion, especially Catholicism?" It is also usually asked by a person who has no real notion what Catholicism is, historically or religiously. The question is based on ignorance and perhaps on bigotry, good old-fashioned anti-Catholic nativism, which is as American as apple pie.

However, the question is worth a response, if only to clarify what religion is and what there is about the Catholic religion that explains its enormous appeal even to men and women who think that the pope is out of touch and that the bishops and the priests are fools. It is also worth answering because of the remarkable tenacity Catholics displayed during the confusing years in which the new wine was bursting the old wineskins and leaving a gosh-awful mess.

Thirty-four percent of Americans were raised Catholic, but only 25 percent are presently Catholic. This rate has remained unchanged since the cohorts born in the 1950s. A third of the defectors are unmarried people who have drifted from the Church to no religious affiliation, a function mostly of the delayed age of marriage. However, most of those return when they marry—though they pass those in the younger generation who are leaving temporarily. Another third live in the Mountain and West Coast states, where defection rates are higher, both for those who have always lived there and for recent migrants. This regional difference in defection (which does not occur among Protestants) seems to be a function of the relative absence of Catholic schools in these regions. (Schools help develop a sense of community loyalty, which seems lower in the West.) The final third is equally distributed among the divorced and remarried and those who leave because of marriage to someone who is not Catholic or has no religious affiliation.[2] It is not immediately clear how the Church should respond to these defections, save perhaps by building more Catholic schools in the West and graciously welcoming home those who have left temporarily.

John Cornwell has argued that the disagreements between the laity and the Vatican portend a schism (Cornwell 2001). Yet one finds in the surveys little inclination and virtually no leadership for a schism.

In a study of mixed marriages, Michael Hout and I found that the proportion of those who were raised Catholic and married others who were raised Catholic has hovered around 63 percent since the cohort born in the 1930s. Despite remarkable changes in the social and economic condition of Catholics and the changes in the Church since the end of World War II, a little less than two-thirds of those who were raised Catholic choose to marry Catholics, an extraordinary display of loyalty to something in the Church. The number of mixed marriages in the Church has increased, because there is now less pressure on spouses who were not raised Catholic to convert at the time of marriage. These mixed marriages account for a decline in the number of marriage converts.[3]

In the same study, we investigated actual defections from the Church since 1972, measured by those who were born Catholic but no longer identify with Catholicism. The proportion has increased through the years, but not greatly (and no more among younger cohorts than among older cohorts). Approximately four out of five who were raised Catholic are still Catholic. Approximately half of those who have left the Church do so in a marriage to someone who is not Catholic. Thus, paradoxically, it would seem that instead of the Catholic party exercising pressure for conversion, as in the past, the pressure now comes from the party who is not Catholic.

Thus Catholics remain in the Church and choose spouses who were born Catholic despite their disagreements with the Vatican, and despite the fact that the kind of reforms they would like to see in the Church do not occur. How can one explain this phenomenon?

Catholics remain Catholic because of the Catholic religious sensibility, a congeries of metaphors that explain what human life means, with deep and powerful appeal to the total person. The argument is not whether Catholics should leave their tradition or whether they stay for the right reasons. The argument is that they do in fact stay because of the attractiveness of Catholic metaphors.

This is an argument that does not make sense to many Catholic leaders and theologians. Metaphors and symbols are just that. What counts is doctrine and institutional structure and discipline. If something is "only a symbol" or "only a metaphor" or "only a story," what good is it? What attractive power can it possibly have for modern, rational humans? If the old rules have collapsed, if the old wineskins have burst, what good are stories, metaphors, and symbols?

You can make a persuasive case against Catholicism if you want. The Church is resolutely authoritarian and often seems to be proud of the fact that it "is not a democracy." It discriminates against women and homosexuals. It tries to regulate the bedroom behavior of married men and women. It tries to impose the Catholic position regarding abortion on everyone. It represses dissent and even disagreement. The Vatican seems obsessed with sex. The pope preaches against birth control in countries with rapidly expanding populations. Catholics often cringe when the local bishop or cardinal pontificates on social policy issues. Bishops and priests are authoritarian and insensitive. Laypeople have no control over how their contributions are spent. Priests are unhappy, and many of them leave the priesthood as soon as they can to marry. The Church has covered up sexual abuse by priests for decades. Now it is paying millions of dollars to do penance for the sexual pleasure of supposedly celibate priests while it seeks to minimize, if not eliminate altogether, the sexual pleasures of married laypeople.

One might contend with such arguments. Research indicates, as we will see subsequently, that priests are among the happiest men in America. The Church was organized in a democratic structure for its first thousand years and could be so organized again. The pope's pronouncements on birth control are not the cause of the population explosion, say, in Mexico. Sexual abuse is not just a problem of the Catholic clergy. But let the charges stand for the sake of the argument. They represent the way many of those who are not Catholic see the Catholic Church, and with some nuances and qualifications, the way many of those inside the Church see the Catholic institution. Nonetheless, this case against Catholicism simply does not compute for most Catholics when they decide whether to leave or stay.

How can this be? the outsider wonders. How can four out of five of those who are born Catholic remain, one way or another, in the Church? Has Catholicism so brainwashed them that they are unable to leave? Or is it possible that those who ask the question misunderstand what Catholicism is?

The answer to the question of why they stay in the Church is that Catholics like being Catholic, as hard as that is for secular professors, journalists, and commentators to understand. For the last thirty years, the hierarchy and the clergy have done just about everything they could to drive the laity out of the Church, and they have not succeeded. It seems unlikely that they will ever drive the stubborn lay folk out, because the lay folk like being Catholic.

But why do they like being Catholic?

First, it must be noted that Americans show remarkable loyalty to their religious heritages. As difficult as it is for members of the academic and media elites to comprehend the fact, religion is important to most Americans. There is no sign that this importance has declined in the last half century (as measured by survey data from the 1940s.) Skepticism, agnosticism, atheism are not increasing in America, as disturbing as this truth might be to the denizens of midtown Manhattan.

Moreover, while institutional authority, doctrinal propositions, and ethical norms are components of a religious heritage— and important components—they do not exhaust the heritage.

Religion is experience, image, and story before it is anything else and after it is everything else. Catholics like their heritage because it has great stories.[4]

If one considers that for much of Christian history the population was illiterate and the clergy semiliterate, and that authority was far away, one begins to understand that the heritage for most people most of the time was almost entirely story, ritual, ceremony, and eventually art. So it has been for most of human history. So it is, I suggest (and my data back me up), even today.

Catholicism has great stories because at the center of its heritage is "sacramentalism," the conviction that God discloses Himself in the objects and events and persons of ordinary life. Hence Catholicism is willing to risk stories about angels and saints and souls in purgatory and Mary the Mother of Jesus and stained glass windows and statues and stations of the cross and rosaries and medals and the whole panoply of images and devotions that were so offensive to the austere leaders of the Reformation. Moreover, the Catholic heritage also has the elaborate ceremonial rituals that mark the passing of the year—Midnight Mass, the Easter Vigil, First Communion, May crowning, Lent, Advent, grammar school graduation, and the festivals of the saints.

Catholicism has also embraced the whole of the human life cycle in Sacraments (with a capital *S*) that provide rich ceremonial settings, even when indifferently administered, for the critical landmarks of life. The Sacrament of Reconciliation (confession that was) and the Sacrament of the Anointing of the Sick (Extreme Unction that was) embed in ritual and mystery the deeply held Catholic story of second chances.

When I was growing up on the West Side of Chicago during the Great Depression I absorbed the charm of the Catholic stories I learned from my parents and from St. Angela parish, its parochial school, and the liturgical cycle, though in those days we hardly knew what liturgy meant. It was an utterly unselfconscious experience. I heard the stories of God and Jesus and Mary and the saints and the angels and especially my own guardian angel, of Christmas and shepherds and the Wise Men and Easter and Ash Wednesday and Advent and Lent and the Souls in Purgatory and the Spirit on Pentecost and the End of the World (in the scary apocalyptic gospels of November and December), and of holy water sprinkled around the house during thunderstorms. My throat was blessed on the Feast of St. Blaise, I prepared for my First Holy Communion, I prayed for the Holy Souls on All Souls Day, I carried the rosary and said it every day, I marched in the Holy Thursday procession while my girl classmates sprinkled flower petals on the church floor between stanzas of the glorious "Pange Lingua." I sang "Bring Flowers of the Rarest" at May crownings. I kissed the wood of the cross on Good Friday. I sang (badly) Christmas carols. I became an altar boy. I watched the colors change with the seasons of the Church year—green, red, white, purple, black. I wore religious medals, lighted votive candles (not very often because we didn't have much money), attended novenas, blessed myself with holy water, made the nine First Fridays, offered up the pain of the dentist's drill for the souls in purgatory. During the war we made novenas for the safe return of the servicemen. Didn't everyone?

Above all I became part of the parish, something that was as natural as breathing air. To live where I lived and to be Catholic meant that I was part of St. Angela parish (with one of the few wooden church buildings left in Chicago). I was fascinated by the priests, whose job it seemed to be to help people and to stand between us and God. I marveled at the nuns, who seemed so kind and gentle and happy (some of them, we would later learn, not yet out of their teens). When we finally graduated from grammar school and many of our young women classmates broke into tears at the drama of pain and joy in that moment, we knew that something very important was slipping away from our lives. I would marvel as a sociologist over the extraordinary genius behind the neighborhood immigrant parish (though our parents were mostly children of immigrants) and its parochial school. Some of the false prophets who were loosed in the confusion of the unchanging Church that changed would loudly proclaim the need to "create community" and were unable to see the enormous community power of the American parish. (Nor did they perceive that community is not as much created as recognized.)

After absorbing the stories and the parish that told the stories and reinforced them, there was no way I could ever be anything but Catholic. No idiocy of Church leadership could possibly drive me out of the Church—and there have been more than a few idiots on the loose during the decades of my life. The remarkable durability of Catholic loyalty during the turbulent years at the beginning of the twenty-first century is in great part, I am convinced, the result of similar experiences, of the sense that once a Catholic, always a Catholic.

I am not suggesting that all of those devotions can or should be restored. I am suggesting that the Eucharist, which is the center of it all, in theological and sociological fact, for most of our people, need not and should not and cannot be separated from the whole aura of metaphors around it. We Catholics grab our metaphors where we can find them and twist them to our use whenever we can. Our imagination is necessarily sacramental because it believes that God is hiding everywhere—like Richard Wilbur's Cheshire smile, which sets us fearfully free—to reveal the love with which He passionately pursues. I admit that the aura of St. Angela in those days seven decades ago was imperfect and sometimes badly understood by many of us. I argue merely that we need something very like it—only better—in our parishes today. The separation of the Eucharist from all the other metaphors in our rain forest of metaphors is artificial, counterproductive, foolish, and even Protestant. It is the genius of Catholicism that it says both-and, instead of either-or.

The "sacramentalism" of the Catholic heritage has also led it to absorb as much as it thinks it can from what it finds to be good, true, and beautiful in pagan religions: Brigid is converted from the pagan goddess to the Christian patron of spring, poetry, and new life in Ireland; Guadalupe is first a pagan and then a Christian shrine in Spain, and then our Lady of Guadalupe becomes the patron of poor Mexicans. This "baptism" of pagan metaphors (done sometimes more wisely than at other times) adds yet another overlay of stories to the Catholic heritage.

The occasionally inaccurate dictum "once a Catholic, always a Catholic" is based on the fact that the religious images and stories of Catholicism are acquired early in life and are tenacious. You may break with the institution, you may reject the propositions, but you cannot escape the images and the stories that contain them.

The Eucharist is a particularly powerful and appealing Catholic ritual, even when it is done badly (as it often is) and especially when it is done well (which it sometimes is). In the Mass we join a community meal of celebration with our neighbors, our family, our friends, those we love. Such an awareness may not be explicitly on the minds of Catholics when they go to church on Saturday afternoon or Sunday morning, but it is the nature of metaphor that those who are influenced by it need not be consciously aware of the influence. In a recent *New York Times*–CBS News poll, 69 percent of Catholics said they attend Mass for reasons of meaning rather than obligation.

When we were in the seminary, we were told that Catholic theology insisted that the Mass was the center of Catholic life. It bound together everything that the Church did and stood for. I don't think we much believed it then, because the argument was so abstract and theoretical. It turns out that we were wrong. Or at least we would be wrong if we were to try to reject the profound importance of the Mass to Catholics. When they return to the Church, often after many years, alienated Catholics insist that it is wonderful to attend Mass again.

Perhaps the Catholic religious sensibility all begins with the Christmas crib. A mother shows her child (perhaps age three) the crib scene. The child loves it (of course) because it has everything she likes—a mommy, a daddy, a baby, animals, shepherds, shepherd children, angels, and men in funny clothes—and with token integration! Who is the baby? the little girl asks. That's Jesus. Who's Jesus? The mother hesitates, not sure of exactly how you explain the communication of idioms to a three-year-old. Jesus is God. That doesn't bother the little girl at all. Everyone was a baby once. Why not God? Who's the lady holding Jesus? That's Mary. Oh! Who's Mary? The mother throws theological caution to the winds. She's God's mommy. Again the kid has no problem. Everyone has a mommy, why not God?

It's a hard story to beat. Later in life the little girl may come to understand that God loves us so much that He takes on human form to be able to walk with us even into the valley of death, and that God also loves us the way a mother loves a newborn babe—which is the function of the Mary metaphor in the Catholic tradition.

It may seem that I am reducing religion to childishness—to stories and images and rituals and communities. In fact, it is in the poetic, the metaphorical, the experiential dimension of the personality that religion finds both its origins and raw power. Because we are reflective creatures, we must also reflect on our religious experiences and stories; it is in the (lifelong) interlude of reflection that propositional religion and religious authority become important, indeed indispensable. But then the religiously mature person returns to the imagery, having criticized it, analyzed it, questioned it, to commit the self once more in sophisticated and reflective maturity to the story.

The Catholic imagination sees God and Grace lurking everywhere and hence enjoys a more gracious and benign repertory of religious symbols than do most other religions. On measures of religious imagery I have developed for national surveys (and call the GRACE scale), Catholics consistently have more "gracious" images of God: they are likelier than others to picture God as a "mother," a "lover," a "spouse," and a "friend" (as opposed to a "father," a "judge," a "master," and a "king"). The story of the life, death, and resurrection of Jesus is the most "grace full" story of all—the story of a God who in some fashion took on human form so that He could show us how to live and how to die, a God who went down into the valley of death with us and promised that death would not be the end.

How do Catholics reconcile such gracious imagery with the often apparently stern and punitive postures of their religious leadership? It must be understood that religious heritages contain many different strains and components, not all of them always in complete harmony with one another. However, in any apparent conflict between images of a gracious God and severe propositional teaching of the leaders of a heritage, the latter will surely lose—as they have in the Catholic revolution.

That which some liturgists and religious educators and feminists dismiss as superfluous and irrelevant is in fact the glue that holds Catholics together, the reason for their loyalty, the most powerful asset with which the leadership could attempt to regain its credibility.

Can I prove from the data that these Catholic images and stories are still relevant in the present post-revolutionary times, perhaps more relevant than they have been in a long time? And that they represent the three main streams of Catholic imagination that I describe in *The Catholic Imagination*—sacramentality, community, and hierarchy?

The most striking evidence is to be found in an item developed by Dean Hoge of the Catholic University, a cafeteria item that seeks to ascertain the most important components of Catholic identity (Hoge et al. 2001). Catholics between the ages of twenty and thirty-nine were asked to rate how essential to their Catholicism were nineteen items, ranging from opposition to abortion and regular Mass attendance to belief that God is present in the Sacraments (see table 7). One might disagree with the wording of some of the items and wish to substitute or include other items, but the broad implication of the findings is clear.

The four items with the highest scores (endorsed by over half of the respondents) were belief in the presence of God in the Sacraments, charitable efforts to help the poor, belief that Christ

Table 7. *Essential Elements of Catholic Identity*
(Percent of Catholics between the ages of 20 and 39)

	Essential to faith
Presence of God in the Sacraments	65%
Charity for the poor	58%
Presence of Christ in the Eucharist	58%
Devotion to Mary the Mother of God	53%
Special presence of God in the poor	52%
Religious orders of priests	48%
Necessity of having a pope	48%
Being a universal Church	45%
Elimination of causes of poverty	42%
Belief that Christ made Peter head of the Church	42%
Regular prayer life	41%
Devotion to the saints	41%
Obligation of weekly Mass	37%
Private confession to a priest	32%
Opposition to abortion	31%
Celibacy of priests	27%
Opposition to death penalty	22%
Belief that only men can be priests	17%
Belief in right of workers to organize	14%

SOURCE: Based on Hoge et al. 2001, p. 201.

is really present in the Eucharist, and devotion to Mary the Mother of Jesus. Thus the strongest components of Catholic identity for young people (most of whom reject the sexual ethic and attend Mass infrequently) are sacramental and communal and (despite Johnson and Wills) Marian. Hierarchy, the third component of the Catholic imagination, is also present, since almost half of the respondents think that having a pope is essential. Whatever the alienation of young people may be on some items of Catholic teaching, their imagination is still Catholic.

Such a survey has yet to be taken of the whole Catholic population in this country, but one has been administered in Ireland, where the findings are similar to those Hoge reports for American young people (Greeley and Ward 2000). In Ireland the young (under thirty) are the ones likeliest to emphasize the importance of devotion to Mary.

Thus the Catholic imagination survives and flourishes in a revolutionary era, utterly undamaged.

Since the findings in Ireland and the United States are similar, one might hazard the guess that they represent emerging new structures of Catholicism, new wineskins that are also ancient (Sacraments, Eucharist, charity, Mary) but now take on a new importance as the wineskins of sex and sin and blind obedience lose their importance and hang empty on the hooks in the wine cellar.

How powerful is that imagination? In *The Catholic Imagination* (2000) I cite many proofs of its importance, two of which are worth noting in the present context. First, Catholics engage in sexual intercourse more often than do other Americans and are more playful in their sex. Second, Catholics who go to church frequently are likelier to attend high culture events (concerts, operas, plays, serious dance). In both cases, the differences can be accounted for by measures of the Catholic imagination.

A new school in the psychology of religion, which bases itself on the so-called attachment theory of psychological maturation, supports my perspective. A happy and playful attachment between mother and baby prepares the child for similar attachments later in life, especially to God, who is in some sense a surrogate mother—an all-powerful source of love and reassurance. Professor Lee A. Kirkpatrick of the College of William and Mary has suggested recently that Catholicism is an especially powerful religious heritage on the imaginative level precisely because it offers so many objects of potential attachment, and the most powerful of all the objects of attachment is the metaphor of Mary the Mother of Jesus representing the mother love of God.

I believe that Kirkpatrick is absolutely right, although some progressive Catholics have tried to play down the role of Mary in the Catholic tradition, lest it offend our ecumenical dialogue partners. Yet who would not find appealing a religion that suggests that God loves us like a mother loves a little child? Who would not be enchanted by a story that suggests that we are, as the Chicago theologian John Shea has argued, not just creatures, not just sinners, but, more than anything, beloved children?

It is the religious sensibility behind fanciful story that explains why Catholics remain Catholic. It might not be *your* religious sensibility. But if you want to understand Catholics—and if Catholics want to understand themselves—the starting point is to comprehend the enormous appeal of that sensibility. It's the stories.

What then are the conclusions I would draw for the Church (and indeed for all religions) from my theory of the religious imagination? I do *not* conclude that religion does not need teaching authority, leadership, creeds, codes, and catechism. Quite the contrary, I insist that all of these functions are needed, though I would wish that my own denomination would exercise these functions better than it does now. Because I focus on the imaginative dimension of religion (which has been neglected for a long

time, though it continues to flourish), it does not follow that I reject the intellectual dimensions of religion. Religion involves
both imagination and intellect (to use a typology that is far from
perfect but is the only one we have). Because I want more regard
for the former, one would be dead wrong to argue that I want less
of the latter.

But I do insist that Catholicism, with the richest repertory of
images and metaphors of any of the world religions, is wasting a
precious and indispensable spiritual resource when it ignores the
religious imagination—and therefore when it ignores the religious experiences of its laypeople. The hierarchy and the clergy
and the quasi clergy (liturgists and "religious educators" in particular) are devoid (with some exceptions) of any sense of the importance of the religious imagination. In fact, they don't know
what it is and their own imaginative creativity—with which
everyone is born—has become little more than a vestigial organ
in the era of beige Catholicism.

They believe that art and stories of any kind are merely gimmicks to gain the attention of the faithful so that they can then
drive home a prosaic and ideological point. You never tell a story,
they seem to think, without explaining its point and drawing conclusions from it. The liturgists, innocent of both taste and creativity (most of them, anyway), replace religious imagery with
cutesy gimmicks that turn the stomach of the ordinary lay folk—
who are almost always too polite or too resigned to protest.
Moreover, liturgists (with my usual bow to the exceptions) have
never seen a liturgy they don't think could be made better by
making it longer and slower—in violation of the genius of the ancient Roman Liturgy, which has always worked on the principles
that you say what you have to say and be done with it and that you

let nothing interfere with flow, the brisk movement of the ceremony (as Dom Gregory Dix pointed out in his magisterial book, *The Shape of the Liturgy*—a volume everyone should read before they are permitted to mess with the Eucharist).

Liturgists, moreover, have absolutely forbidden Gregorian Chant in church, an ancient and glorious tradition, and replaced it whenever possible with sickening guitar music.[5] Chant records meanwhile become international best-sellers because the music is so beautiful, so deeply religious, and, in some cases, so easy to sing. Greeley's First Law: When everyone else discovers something, the Catholic Church has just abandoned it.[6] I do not want plainsong to dominate the Church's worship (as it once did, though usually it was badly sung plainsong), but I think it is monstrous folly to exclude it completely.

Liturgical art and music are in serious disrepair in the contemporary Church, both because it takes a while to develop a tradition after it has been dormant for half a millennium and because Catholic leaders want everything both quick and cheap.

Church architects, for some reason that escapes me, seem to have concluded that a "modern" church is necessarily one that looks not like a Catholic church but like a Quaker meeting hall. We must be brave, they say, even if it means offending the laity who have paid for the church (and for the previous one, if the issue is a remodeling job). The laity, it would seem, have neither good taste nor religious sensibility. "Liturgy committees" are lectured about what a "liturgically correct" church is and, their minds filled with ideology, approve the architect's and the pastor's plans for a new church or a remodeling project. If the rest of the parish is given a chance to vote on the project (a rare enough event), they usually turn it down flat.

Many such "modern" churches assume that the exuberance of the older style of Catholic churches—dark stained-glass windows, a multitude of statues, a faint smell of incense, and votive candles everywhere—is tasteless and old fashioned. A church is only in good taste when it looks like a Protestant church. But such an assumption is surely invalid. What's wrong with saints, the mother of Jesus, stained glass, and votive candles? Why must the tradition be wiped out completely? Cannot one build a modern church that "looks like a Catholic church" (as many laity wonder)? By which they mean, in effect, is it not possible to have a modern church that integrates the Catholic tradition of exuberant churches?

Why not indeed?

The religious imagination will flourish again in the Catholic tradition only when the Church resumes its traditional patronage of the fine and the lively arts. It has been a long way from, let us say, the Sistine Chapel, the Stanza of Raphael, the Pietà, the baroque Jesuit churches, Fra Angelico, Palestrina, Notre Dame de Paris, and the book of Kells. And all that way has been down hill. Fine art is no longer an absolute necessity for a Church with a sacramental imagination; it has become at best a luxury we can ill afford and at worst a dangerous temptation to pride. Artists, musicians, story tellers, poets are treated with contempt, paid poorly, and lied about. Rarely will priests or bishops or a pope trust fourth-rate surgeons when they must have an operation (well, maybe the pope does, given the poor quality of the medical care he receives). Yet they all want art (in the wide sense of the word) that is quick, cheap, and will not trouble the Vatican.

If you are dealing with men and women who are scarcely Christian, who need to be "evangelized," you must pound home doctrinal truth because, you assume, there is no religious imagination at all. If your people are pagans, of what use is the popular tradition of Catholicism? Indeed, is it not little more than an accretion of pagan superstitions? Why let them have votive lights when they can't recite the Ten Commandments? Or they don't know the difference between a secular and religious order priest? Why permit Midnight Masses at Christmas when they are not raising their kids properly? Why worry about making the baptism ceremony a rich and exciting experience when they come in off the street and expect you to baptize their child and they go to Mass only a couple of times a year?

Neither in art (fine or lively) nor in the life of the average parish is much attention paid to the two greatest resources of Catholicism—the imaginative tradition and the spirituality of the lay folk that correlates with that tradition. The new and dreary *Catechism of the Catholic Church* is a perfect example of what Church leaders think religion is.[7] While I am not repudiating the catechism, I am arguing that the popular tradition, the tradition of story and image and experience and ritual, is even more important, though always subject to critique by propositional religion.

I am urging as a challenge a Catholicism that is far more aware of its imaginative tradition and has much greater respect for it. In practice this means that a typical parish should be exuberant and celebratory in its rituals, all of its rituals, from blessing a medal to the Mass. Its approach should be sensitive, compassionate, open, eager to listen to the experiences of the faithful. The Mass itself should have the highest quality homilies, readings, music, ceremonies. It should be the kind of *représentation collectif* from which the congregants depart happy, smiling, exhilarated, renewed—instead of grim, angry, bored, and depressed. If one does not see many smiles on the faces of the faithful after Mass, something is profoundly wrong.

Catholics stay in the Church despite their disagreements with the Vatican, despite the confusion of this revolutionary era because they like being Catholic, and they like being Catholic because of the metaphors, the images, and the stories. The Catholic imagination not only keeps them in the Church, it affects their lives, more perhaps than doctrinal prose.

TEN

Priests

Priests were the officers in the Catholic revolution. Their changes in attitude toward birth control, masturbation, and divorce occurred at the same time as the revolutionary effervescence spread among the laity. Their change in attitude may have been caused by the lay change. It is likelier that they supported and reinforced the idea that laypeople should follow their consciences. As leaders of the revolution they should be pleased with lay independence, which appeared so suddenly. Priests also are responsible for the emergence of beige Catholicism and the new authoritarian pragmatism. The priests who persisted in the beginning of the revolution are probably not the same as those who are promoting the imposition of new and utterly illegal rules with the help of their parish staff. Perhaps some of the new rules have come into being as an attempt to impose a new order on a chaotic Church.

The 1972 NORC report to the bishops showed that men were leaving the priesthood because they were not happy in it and their unhappiness made celibacy difficult. When it became possible to marry, they did so. Claims made by some of the resigning priests that they were the most mature and most courageous of priests turned out to be self-serving. Moreover, only about a quarter of those leaving would have been willing to return to the work they had previously performed if they could do so as married priests.

The priesthood, however, has paid a high price for its revolutionary leadership. Its image has been badly scarred by the complaints of some of those who left and more recently by the pedophile scandals. Because of these phenomena, vocations to the priesthood have fallen drastically.

Since 1970, then, American priests have been caught between two forces. On one side stand the laity, of whom they often do not have a very high opinion and whose unreasonable demands they resent, but whose freedom of moral decision making they accept. On the other side stands the institutional Church, from many of whose moral teachings they dissent, though they generally approve of the performance of its leaders. Such are the paradoxical conclusions one could draw from two 1994 studies (both based on representative probability samples) of the priesthood (Greeley 1994). One study was conducted for the National Federation of Priest Councils (NFPC) by the Life Cycle Institute of the Catholic University of America, the other by the *Los Angeles Times* under the direction of the late John Brennan. The former was based on 1,186 respondents (a 71 percent response rate) and the latter on 2,061 respondents (a 42 percent response rate). Insofar as the two surveys address themselves to the same or similar questions, their findings are the same—a phenomenon that enhances the credibility of both.

The findings of the two projects may be summarized under four headings.

1. The much-discussed morale crisis in the priesthood does not exist.

The NFPC study reports that priests have the same levels of emotional well-being as married men of the same age and education. Moreover, only 1 percent say they are likely to leave the priesthood and 6 percent more are uncertain about their future, while 72 percent say they will definitely not leave the priesthood. (This is a change from the 1970 finding [NORC 1972], doubtless because in 1994 many of those who had thought about leaving had actually done so.) In the *Times* data, 2 percent say they are very likely to leave the priesthood and 4 percent somewhat likely; 87 percent say they are very unlikely to leave.

In the latter study, 4 percent say they are very dissatisfied with their life as a priest and 9 percent more say they are somewhat dissatisfied. Fifty-six percent are very satisfied. Seventy percent say they would definitely choose to be a priest again and 20 percent more say they probably would so choose. Fifty-four percent say that life as a priest is better than they expected; 36 percent say it is as expected, and only 10 percent find that it is worse than expected.

These findings are not completely surprising. The 1970 survey of American priests by the National Opinion and Research Center (NORC 1972) displayed similar levels of emotional well-being and psychological maturity. Moreover, work done in the Archdiocese of Chicago by the Reverend Thomas Nestor at Loyola University showed that priests on the average scored higher on most measures of work and life satisfaction than did comparable samples of married laymen (and lower on none of the measures). A. W. Richard Sipe has argued that the 1970 NORC study is now out of date. However, he lacked both probability samples and lay comparison groups to sustain his theses, and his contentions are belied by these more recent studies.

If there is in fact no morale crisis, why do so many priests think there is? Perhaps the explanation is that most priests are themselves happy and satisfied in the priesthood but think that their fellow priests are not happy, possibly because the agenda of clerical discussions tend to be set by those who are dissatisfied.

2. *Celibacy does not seem to be the problem that it is often alleged to be.*

The *Times* survey indicates that only 4 percent of priests would definitely marry if the Church approved, and 13 percent more would probably marry, while half would definitely not marry (less than a quarter of those under 45 say they would definitely or probably marry). Only 14 percent of the respondents in the NFPC study say that celibacy is a serious problem for them personally. Dr. Sipe's allegation of widespread psychosexual problems in the priesthood is not sustained by the data reported here.

Why would most priests not marry even if they could? There are two possible answers: Either they are inadequate as males and do not find women attractive or they realize the importance of celibacy in their life and ministry. Since in other respects they seem to be happy and functioning men, the latter seems the more plausible explanation. One would like to know more about the experience of celibacy of such men—happy, effective males—and hear theological reflection on it. In the present anti-celibacy climate, however, that is not likely to happen.

If celibacy is not so serious a problem as some have claimed, why then does the image persist that it is an impossible burden?

Perhaps because those for whom it was or is a burden are the only ones who discuss the issue.

In light of these first two findings, why is there a vocation shortage in the Church? The 1979 NORC study of young Catholics concluded that the shortage resulted in great part from a lack of recruitment efforts by priests and mothers. One suspects that priests do not recruit, despite their own happiness and their ability to cope (relatively) with celibacy, because of their mistaken image of how their fellow priests feel. Unfortunately, the NFPC report does not address itself to the subject of vocational recruiting.

3. Large proportions of priests do not accept the official teachings of the Church about moral behaviors that are considered always wrong.

While 80 percent believe that euthanasia is always wrong and 69 percent think that suicide is always wrong and 68 percent make that judgment about abortion, only 56 percent think that homosexual sex is always wrong and 50 percent that premarital sex is always wrong. Forty-seven percent disapprove of surrogate mothers, 35 percent of condoms to protect from AIDS, 28 percent of masturbation, and 25 percent of artificial birth control. Many more, of course, believe that some of these actions are "often" wrong. The point is that these responses would surely not be judged adequate by the Vatican, which deems all of these actions always wrong.

Fifty-two percent of the priests in the *Times* study think that masturbation is seldom or never wrong, 48 percent think that birth control is seldom or never wrong. Twenty percent think that homosexual sex is seldom or never wrong and 11 percent think that premarital sex is seldom or never wrong.

What accounts for this dissent from official teaching, especially in the face of the rigorous stands taken on moral subjects by the Papacy? Have priests succumbed to the materialism and secularism and "hypersexuality" of the age? Or is their dissent based on a systematic belief that is at odds with that which shapes the official teaching? The data suggest it is the latter.

To test the question, I speculate that the opposition to official teaching might be based on a mixture of three currents of thought and feeling that exist in western society today—a positive valuation of sexuality, more sensitivity to women, and greater respect for the freedom of the laity to make their own moral decisions (a respect manifested by half the priests despite their apparent low opinion of lay folk). To measure the positive valuation of sexuality, I used the admittedly crude indicator that a respondent would probably or certainly marry if he were free to do so (though patently, many priests who would not marry nonetheless evaluate human sexuality positively). For sensitivity to women I used a factor composed of support for the ordination of women, concern for the low status of women religious, desire that sexism be declared a sin, and belief that ministry to women ought to be improved.

These three variables constituted a very powerful model that explains more than half the variance in the moral attitudes of priests. The strongest of the three variables was respect for the freedom of the laity to make their own moral decisions. Next came sensitivity to women and then positive valuation of sexuality. The power of these factors was not a function of a "liberal" religious bias. Even when self-descriptions as religiously "liberal," "moderate," or "conservative" were entered into the equation, the three variables in the model had virtually the same impact.

My conclusion: A well-elaborated ideology accounts for

priestly dissent. American priests tend to value human sexuality, lay freedom, and the dignity of women. The Vatican of course does not reject any of these values, but it interprets them very differently than do American priests. It would be unwise, in the absence of similar studies in other countries, to say that this ideology exists only in the United States. Surely the anecdotal evidence available from other English-speaking countries would suggest that the situation there does not differ markedly from that in the United States. Moreover, previously cited studies done by the International Social Survey Program of sexual attitudes in some thirty countries show that the attitude of Catholic laity toward sexual ethics is similar in all countries.

Patently, this dissent is a serious problem for the Church. It does not seem likely that the problem will be resolved by statements from Rome or from bishops, by the removal of theologians, by the banning of books, by the transformation of seminary faculties, or by the publication of new catechisms. The dissent of priests on issues of sexual morality is "principled." I do not mean that the principles are correct; I mean only that they seem to be principles on which many or most priests (depending on the issue) are not ready to yield.

4. Despite this dissent, most priests give Church leadership moderately high marks.

Eighty-three percent approve "strongly" or "somewhat" of the job performance of the present pope and 72 percent of the job performance of their own bishops. Forty-one percent think that the pope is too conservative on moral issues and 22 percent think their bishop is too conservative on these issues. But how can this strong approval of the pope and the bishop coexist with a willingness to reject official moral teachings? (This question is a variant of that constantly propounded by the media about all Catholics: How can they like the pope and reject his teachings?)

A hint of an answer to that puzzle can be found. Nine out of ten of those who think that birth control is always sinful also "strongly" support the pope. More than eight out of ten of those who think it is seldom or never sinful do not strongly approve of the pope's job performance. But six out of ten of those who hedge in their answer—by saying that birth control is "often" sinful (a lukewarm answer of which the pope would surely not approve)— also strongly approve of the pope's job performance. The hedgers or fudgers who are not willing to say that birth control is always wrong nor that it is never wrong are those who approve (at least "somewhat") of the pope and at the same time dissent—albeit cautiously—from his teaching.

It is not my function as a sociologist to approve or disapprove of this "liberalism" on sexual matters among priests. It is my function rather to report it honestly so that others may discuss it—and perhaps worry about it. One does not arrive at moral principles by taking surveys. One arrives only at a rough approximation of social reality.

Priests saw the wineskins bursting and rushed in to save the situation by counseling the laity of the need to base decisions on their own consciences. They thus reinforced and extended the effervescence of the revolutionary movement. It would appear that they continued to play the same role even in the late 1990s.

PART II

The Search for New Wineskins

ELEVEN

Recovering the Catholic Heritage

The Catholic analogical imagination is . . . fragile—it could be
lost if it is not cultivated in successor generations.

Terrence Tilley

In the remaining chapters of this essay, I turn away from analysis
to discuss the implications for the Church of that analysis.[1] I stand
by the integrity of my data and the soundness of my analysis. My
policy reflections go beyond my analysis but seem to me to flow
from it.

John Shea has written somewhere that it is the Catholic genius
to search in the trash cans and the junkyards of history for forgotten symbols that might still have value. Thus if one tries to recover some of the potentially useful and valuable symbols of the
heritage, one must explore the images and stories and metaphors,
the art and beauty of the Catholic past.[2]

Catholics are different, not completely different, but still different. We belong to a sacramental Church and hence are a sacramental people, different to some extent from those who are less sacramental than we are. Since the Second Vatican Council, false prophecy, not based on the Council itself but on illegitimate readings of it, has preached that Catholics should abandon their differences and become just like everyone else. In the post-revolutionary decades this false prophecy has infected only some elements of the Church's elite—priests, nuns, teachers, parish staff members, journalists, and intellectuals (or would-be intellectuals). The ordinary laypeople, who pretty much don't count in the fads and fashions that seem to sweep in on every new tide, are relatively immune to it. The false prophets are not evil people, quite the contrary, they are virtuous and well intentioned.[3] They are, however, poorly educated and tend to substitute enthusiasm for a mature understanding of Catholicism and its heritage, a heritage that sees that God's grace is everywhere and that indeed everything is grace. The sacramental imagination cannot be replaced by a mix of pseudo-fourth-century liturgy and politically correct social attitudes. Whatever might emerge from such a mélange, it is not Catholicism.

A heritage, or perhaps more precisely a cultural heritage, is a tool kit, a set of paradigms that suggest attitudes and behavior appropriate as responses to the problems and opportunities of life. Usually a heritage is subconscious and unreflective. The problem of defining and describing a heritage is complex and intricate. In this chapter I specifically address myself to some of the responses that affect Catholic attitudes toward creation, especially those called the sacramentals.

The issue is not restoration, either of the variety preached by far right or more moderate men in the Roman Curia. The Catholicism of the 1940s and 1950s cannot be restored and should not be even if it could be. The conciliar projects—liturgical reform, ecumenism, biblical renewal, respect for the modern world, collegiality—are not to be abandoned. (Indeed, one might wonder if instead of being tried and found wanting, collegiality was found hard and not tried.) Rather, the issue is whether, in their haste to adjust to the postconciliar world, Church persons may have jettisoned much of what was both distinctive and precious in the Catholic sacramental heritage.

An example of a discarded element of the Catholic heritage: plainsong, which is a rich and powerful element of Catholic culture that has flourished for at least fifteen centuries. It has recently been celebrated on best-selling CDs. Yet liturgists have virtually banished it from Catholic worship on the grounds that there is no place for it in the postconciliar liturgy.

I am tempted to ask who says so. You can't sing chant with English words, I am told. I'm not so sure about that, but I'll concede the point for the sake of the argument. Yet one hardly becomes an advocate of the teachings of the Society of Pius X or the Society of Pius V if one says that on some occasions a congregation might sing the "Kyrie," the "Sanctus," and the "Agnus Dei" in their original languages (Greek, Hebrew, and Latin) in antiphonal mode with a skilled schola cantorum. To suggest a revival of chant is not to reject (as Cardinal Ratzinger apparently does) the liturgical reform of Paul VI or the documents of the Council, or even developments in Church music (such as these may be) since the Council. Rather, it is to advocate the recovery of a tradition of great beauty that has been part of the Catholic heritage for ages. (One might even let Mozart back into the Eucharist on occasion.)

As I stated earlier, it is the genius of Catholicism that it can say both-and instead of either-or. Can we not have *both* the liturgical reforms of the Council *and* chant, for example? If we can't, then why not and who says we can't?

Plainsong is not of the essence of the Catholic heritage. It could be abandoned forever and Catholicism would still be Catholicism, albeit marginally poorer in its beauty. But why abandon it? Why should we not strive to recover it and the many rejected metaphors ("sacraments" with a small *s*) in Catholicism's rain forest of metaphors? If something is beautiful and hints of God's loving presence in the world, the question is not why we should recover it but why we abandoned it in the first place. Why not sing the "Pange Lingua" on Holy Thursday?

Beige Catholicism—Catholicism stripped of much of its beauty, its rain forest of metaphors denuded, in a manic and thoughtless effort to be just like everyone else. The beige Catholicism of today is somehow trapped between the solemn and empty rituals and the pervasive superstitions of the so-called confident Church and the bare bones of low-church Protestantism—not quite Catholic but not really Protestant either.

The Catholic imagination, as David Tracy has argued theologically and as I have demonstrated empirically, is sacramental. It sees the Ultimate lurking in the Everyday, in the bits and pieces of everyday life. God discloses Himself in water, food and drink, sexual love, birth, death, the touch of a friendly hand, the pale glow of the sun on a frozen winter lake, the sight of a familiar face long unseen, a Puccini aria, reconciliation after a quarrel, in all the beautiful events and people and places of human life. When I'm asked how the Catholic imagination differs from the Protestant ("Dialectical" in Fr. Tracy's word), I reply that we have angels and saints and souls in purgatory and statues and stations of the cross and votive candles and religious medals and crucifixes and rosaries and Mary the Mother of Jesus and First Communions and Candlemas and Ash Wednesday and May crownings and Midnight Masses and pilgrimages and relics and they don't. These days I realize that we don't have most of those things anymore either. Our elite, our teachers, our experts, our professorate have banished them so that we can be more like everyone else, more Protestant, that is. It is a peculiarly one-sided notion of ecumenism in which we are asked to abandon the riches of our heritage to keep other people happy. If some Protestants are offended by the statues in our churches, and even today many of them are, they don't have to enter them, or they at least should be prepared to listen to our explanation of them as an explanation and not a defense.

Neither the Protestant nor the Catholic imagination is without risks. The former risks a God-forsaken universe, the latter superstition and folk religion. Many of the Catholic elite are only too eager to denude our rain forest of metaphors because, particularly in our Calvinist American society, they are more than a little ashamed of them.

It might be said that all this "stuff" that used to litter our churches is not essential to Catholicism, not even really part of Catholic doctrine. These are accidentals, derivatives that have been added to the heritage over the centuries and are not important. God, Trinity, incarnation, Church, pope, service of the poor—these are the essentials of our faith. However, such an argument confuses the way we first encounter our religious heritage and its stories with the way the doctrines are systematically arranged by theologians and catechism writers. Stories come first, then theological and catechetical systematization, which enables us to critique the stories, and then finally, in what Paul Ricoeur calls the "second naivete," we return to the stories. Religion begins with stories and ends with stories.

My pastor in Tucson has retrieved the Feast of the Epiphany, which was lost in the games played with it after the Council. The festival of Twelfth Night, Little Christmas, Mother's Christmas, the bridge between East and West has been reduced to a Sunday after itself. So he has a vast parish dinner that night for all the people who have worked in the ministry of the parish, all 350 of them, and serves a dinner catered by the best Mexican American restaurant in Tucson. Free!

He also divided the Rite of Christian Initiation of Adults (RCIA) into those who had been baptized and those who had not, an appropriate decision because the RCIA is technically only for unbaptized. The baptized Christians went through a ten-week course of faith affirmation (which he taught himself, a practice that is breaking all the rules). He discovered that many of them could hardly wait to get a rosary, because this was proof that they were really going to be Catholics. So he made distribution of rosaries an integral part of the preparation for being accepted in the Church.

The rosary! Hasn't that been banned by the liturgists? Isn't it a holdover from medieval superstitions? Shouldn't we give up the nervous fingering of the beads of the grandmas and babushkas?[4]

One of the great arenas for the study of comparative religion are the taxicabs in large American cities. One sees in them every variety of prayer bead under heaven. Why should we give up ours?

We did give up fish on Friday, one of the great definitions of Catholic identity, for no good reason of which I am aware. We were probably contemptuous of it as preconciliar. Despite the thinking of some bishops that all you have to do to re-create a metaphor is make a rule, that won't work. A mentality has to emerge among Catholics that we do some things not because they are a rule but because Catholics do them, because in fact they like to do them.

The bishops didn't understand that there was a via media between saying it was a sin to eat meat on Friday and saying it was not a sin. That middle ground is to tell the laity that they won't go to hell for eating meat on Friday, but it is the sort of thing Catholics don't do because fish on Friday is an old symbol of our faith, not the most important symbol surely, but one that was not so long ago very visible.

It is hard for bishops to imagine the middle ground between sin and non-sin.

Epiphany, the rosary, Friday abstinence, statues, Holy Days— none of them are essential, but until we find better metaphors for the presence of God's personal love in the world, we would do well to conserve them instead of tossing them into the ash can of history.

Perhaps the most powerful of all our metaphors is that of the Madonna, the story that the One who is behind the Cosmos, the One who ignited the big bang is something like the love of a mother for her newborn child. It would be difficult to find a hint in the conciliar documents that Mary was no longer fashionable. But in sad truth we hear very little about her these days, probably for fear that Marian devotion would offend our separated brothers and sisters. English historian Eamon Duffy, in a powerful Meyer lecture, lamented that theologians have written little about Mary in the last thirty years. I suspect that they don't for fear of reaction in their guilds (and of feminist ideologues like Elizabeth Johnson) to such theological reflection—or to theological reflection on any of the other metaphors from our rain forest that still manage to survive. Theologians today write mostly for the fellow members of their guilds and especially for the ideological thought police who dominate the guilds. Theology is now politics, though most theologians are quite incapable of delivering a pack of starved vampires to a blood bank.

Could not the Mary symbol be rearticulated as representing the maternal love of God for the creatures, we little children, the crying babies to whom God has given life and nurturance? Indeed, is this not the prima facie meaning of the symbol? Why do we need to pretend that Mary isn't part of our heritage? Why do contemporary Catholic theologians ignore her like Victorian novelists ignored sex? Why does she embarrass us? Why have we left her to those who wish to multiply titles or those who pursue gnostic interpretations in private revelations?

The trouble with theologians, among other things, is that they believe a description of a problem from a perspective they call theological is in and of itself a solution to the problem. The rain forest is not politically correct, you see. If it still survives, they tell us, it will not last another generation.

Purgatory has been swept away. If you check the internet listings for purgatory, you find merely repetitions of the catechism answers of fifty years ago in which the fires of purgatory are distinguished from the fires of hell. Can we not do better than that?

D. M. Thomas, in his wonderful novel *The White Hotel*, suggests that purgatory is a place where our task is to straighten out the messes we have made of our human relationships. This seems like a legitimate exegesis of the purgatory story, and a reassuring and encouraging explanation of its pain, which is also a joy. We can wisely pray for those in purgatory that they work through their problems and ask their help that we anticipate the pains and the joys of purgatory by striving for reconciliation in this life.

I offer this interpretation merely as one possibility. However, any attempt to take seriously the Catholic heritage that does not take into account the purgatory element in that heritage (even if as a place with that name it harkens back only to thirteenth-century Ireland) is gravely deficient. Who are we to offer our pains for, whether they be from terminal cancer or a toothache? For whom are we to pray if the dead really cannot profit from our prayers? Do we even realize that a heritage that recommends and reinforces praying for the dead is a heritage that is both rich and benign?[5]

Make no mistake about it, however: as a sacramental religion that believes in the presence of a loving God in God's creation, we will inevitably become a heritage in which sacramentals (small *s*) abound. You may wipe them out as cleanly as they have been wiped from churches that follow the bishops' ill-advised advice that the only symbols of moment in the Church should be the altar, the ambo, and the font. But once the present crop of sacramentals has been cleaned away, our people will invent new ones, because they are a sacramental people. In fact, they may reinvent many of the old ones, most notably the Madonna image.

Get rid of one set of stories, as the false prophets would have us do, there will follow another set of stories about the abundant presence of God's superabundant love. Clear away the rain forest and a new one will grow up. Strip the trees and new foliage and branches will grow. The problem then is not to rid ourselves of statues and crucifixes and medals and angels and saints and holy water and the poor souls and Mary. The problem rather is how to reinterpret and rearticulate some of our stories so they represent the authentic story and do not degenerate into superstition, folk religion, and magic. Nine Fridays will not, on the record, guarantee the presence of a priest when we need one. But they will reinforce our conviction that God watches over us in life and in the moment of death as beloved children.

Very few people—theologians, teachers, spiritual writers—have any interest in this task or any awareness that it is important. They seem unpersuaded that hard-core politically correct ideology (of the right or the left) is an inadequate substitute for the richness of our heritage. We are not Quakers (though we can learn from them), we are not Bible Christians (though we can learn from them too), we are not even Lutherans (though we have learned much from them). We are Catholics. No useful purpose is served by pretending that we are not. We know or can understand, if we are so taught, that the statues represent stories of God's love worked out in some of his favorite people. That others may not choose to understand what we mean by this conviction is perhaps at this stage inevitable, but it does not follow that we should abandon this conviction (or hide it) just to keep them happy. Or that our treasonous clerks should try to pretend that we don't have statues any more. We decided against the iconoclast temptation long ago, even if we understand that the iconoclasts may have had a point.

One of the great sacramental moments in contemporary cinema is when the Meryl Streep character in the film *Ironweed* finds under the statue of St. Joseph, the patron of a happy death, the ten dollars that will shape her lonely death into a happy one. Obviously William Kennedy, who wrote the screenplay as well as the novel, knew the happy death story, because the statue of St. Joseph is a visual that did not appear in the book. Rather, in the book he says, "She was searching for grace." I realize how pervasive Robert Barron's beige Catholicism is when I point this out to his generation of Catholics and they don't know the happy death story.

Richard Dreyfuss and Steven Spielberg knew little about the angels of the Lord, the Malek Yahweh, representing God's personal tender care for each of us. Yet when they chose Audrey Hepburn to play that role in *Always* (as a reprise of Lionel Barrymore in the original *A Guy Named Joe*), they understood both God and angels much better than do our contemporary demythologizers. They cast the incomparable Hepburn to play God in what would be her last role before she joined God. Just as we have relinquished Mary to the Mariological enthusiasts, so we have turned over the angels to the cultists of the occult (behavior of which the angels, I am convinced, strongly disapprove).

Our stories are out there, you see, and still being used, whether we like it or not. They are good stories. They demand to be used. At least we can strive to assure that they are used properly by striving to understand them better.

There are four special dimensions we must consider as we begin the task of retrieving the Catholic heritage.

1. The sacramental imagination has not completely disappeared from the lives of the faithful, no matter how little we have tended it in the last third of the century. The task in great part will be to surface it again for their formal consideration. This will involve their being much more conscious and explicit than they are about what it means to be Catholic and how we differ, inevitably and deeply, from others, without at all claiming superiority over them. We make the sign of the cross with holy water when we enter the church to recall the graces of our baptism, to understand that God's love for us lurks in life-giving water, and to remind ourselves that we are entering the house where in a special way God is present. Most people know that or knew it once. Yet they need to hear often that Catholics believe not that water is magical, but that there is grace in water. Catholics know that in some way they are different. It is the task of teachers in this time of transition to remind them that we are different because we are sacramental, because we believe that grace is everywhere.

2. *We must discern what elements of the heritage may require more emphasis than others.* It is not necessary that every private devotion, every pious custom of the past be revived. Novenas, it seems, had run out before the Council, perhaps because there were too many of them and the prayers were too odd and the promises too automatic. On the other hand, visits to the Blessed Sacrament (a wonderful way to end a novel, as John P. Marquand found in his *So Little Time*) disappeared because priests began to lock up churches, regardless of the fact that there are now many security devices that would permit the church to stay open for those who want to "drop in and say a prayer."[6]

3. *We must learn how to exegete our stories so that the risks of superstition, folk religion, and idolatry are less serious than they may have been at some times and in some places not so long ago.* Sacramentals are not instruments of magic that control God and by the use of which we can manipulate God into doing what we want Him to

do. Lourdes water is a form of prayer for God's maternal love. It does not force God to cure someone who is ill, though it may remind the sick person of God's grace. Once a candle burning in church ceases to be a reminder to us of our prayer when we are not in church and becomes an automatic guarantee of the desired outcome of our prayer, then we have left behind Catholicism and have entered paganism. When we walk in and out of church on All Souls Day, collecting plenary indulgences by the sackful, we may amuse the God who has to be a comedienne or She wouldn't have produced such strange creatures as us, but we do not constrain Her to be any more merciful than She already is.

Recovering and rearticulating our symbols is part of the task of religious maturation, the journey from what Ricoeur calls the "first naivete" to the "second naivete." It constitutes the phase of "criticism" in our religious growing up in which we analyze and unpack our symbols, take them apart to see what they mean, and then put them back together again. It is that part of our journey in which we progress from the simple faith of the child to the sophisticated faith of the adult, from making the sign of the cross with holy water when we enter the church because everyone else does to understanding that we are renewing, however briefly and however occasionally, the exchange of promises made at baptism. Perhaps one can say that American Catholicism is at a time when it is collectively struggling toward the "second naivete."

4. We must represent our sacramentality in ways that emphasize and celebrate its beauty. As I will argue subsequently, of the three transcendentals, the Good, the True, and the Beautiful, the last is the first we encounter. The Beautiful attracts us. We examine it and see that it is Good. Having examined Goodness, we determine that it is True. The beautiful, Pope John Paul has said, is the portal to God. The Catholic Church for much of its existence has presided over and preserved traditions of beauty, indeed one might say of exuberant beauty. Yet in contemporary puritan, pragmatic American Catholicism, the beautiful is not only the last and the least of the transcendentals, it has become an appendage, at most a useful option, that is, when it is not a waste of money or a temptation to sensuality. Some groups in the American Catholic community have come with brilliant traditions of beauty. The Germans created gorgeous churches, the Irish built schools and used the school hall for Mass. Whatever might be said of past practices, there is no longer an excuse for omitting beauty from our sacramental (small *s* or capital *S*) life. If we are to use school halls as chapels, they have to be beautiful school halls. By beautiful I do not mean cute or pretty or sweet, but possessing the kind of hint of the transcendent that tears a hole in the fabric of ordinary life and lets grace pour in.

The stories contained in the metaphors often have a propensity to grow and develop. Thus the monsignor's idea that the Epiphany was a good time to feed those who served the parish may well have been based on the Irish custom of Mother's Christmas or Women's Christmas, in which the servers are themselves served at the end of the Christmas season, as perhaps one more manifestation of Jesus' love as contained in the *epiphanos* festival.

In the newly immigrant American society (9 percent of Americans are foreign born), there will be other systems of sacramentality than the one assumed here. Thus Sister Nancy Wellmeir tells the sad story of the Mayan-speaking Guatemalans who were unwelcome in a Latino parish because their languages and customs were different. Pluralism is a hard lesson to learn.

Some theologians argue that in addition to sacramentality, Catholicism also emphasizes community and hierarchy. Surely this is true, though one could also say that to see grace in community and leadership is simply an application of sacramentality. Grace is everywhere, hence in community and leadership, indeed especially so. The false prophets are devoted to community, or at least to the word, but it has often come to mean communities that they have convened and dominate or communities that exist only by extension of the meaning of the word. They have little time for the unique American Catholic community of neighborhood/parish/school. They announce that the day of the neighborhood parish is over and campaign on every possible occasion and on whatever possible pretense for the end of Catholic schools, which they argue are after all really part of the preconciliar Church, a Church that was afraid to be like everyone else. When one suggests to them that the parish school is sacramental—revelatory of the presence of God in a specific time and place—they complain about Catholic schools they have known or about those who do not attend Catholic schools, either because they cannot or will not. They do not perceive that parochial schools, despite the beige Catholicism that has infected some of them in recent decades, are the creators and bearers of a distinctive sacramental culture, a toolbox of attitudes and responses to life and its problems. Even if they did perceive that reality, they would not think it very important. On the contrary, they argue, with a genius for the cliché buzzwords that substitute for thought, that the parochial schools are an obstacle to evangelization.

A certain priest informed me that the inner city schools for African Americans should be closed because they were not effective evangelization, since few of the students converted to

Catholicism. That the schools might do work of both justice and charity was not important in comparison with their failure to make converts. In China there were once converts who were called "rice Christians": they became Christian so that they would be given rice to eat. In the United States today, we apparently do not have enough Catholic school Christians to justify their ministry. No argument against Catholic schools is too mindless not to be used against them.

In my research on the persistence of religion in Europe (Greeley 2003), I discovered that religion survived most effectively when it was linked with a pervasive religious culture that had been shaped by it and continued to be supported by it—as in Catholic countries like Ireland, Italy, Spain, Poland, and Slovakia, and in Catholic regions like those in Switzerland, and Protestant regions like those in Switzerland, Slovakia, and Latvia. In countries like the Netherlands, where religion was propped up for many years by a political structure, it collapsed almost overnight. After World War II a plague of French "religious sociologists" and their American acolytes dismissed American devotion as "cultural Catholicism." The implication was that religion had to forsake the support of a religious culture or subculture to be authentic. For all their certainty (French sociologists never lack certainty), they misunderstood that religion is part of culture and that the relationship between religion and the rest of a country's cultural system is never neutral.

There is a strong Catholic religious subculture in this country, one that has to a considerable extent been able to resist serious damage from the attacks of first of all the Protestant host culture, and more recently religion-hating secularism. Now the false prophets of beige Catholicism want to destroy it because it prevents Catholics from being like everyone else. There are many different institutions that have created the distinctive American Catholic subculture, among them Catholic schools and Catholic colleges and universities, all of which seem to be experiencing an identity crisis as the conventional wisdom demands that they become like all other educational institutions.

Many priests and educators have chanced on the bright idea of combining parochial schools into "regional academies" and are surprised that enrollment declines once parish identification is removed. Why, they wonder, as they close schools and eventually parishes, do people have so much loyalty to parish communities? After generations of effort to build up loyal parochial communities, they now seem eager to tear them down. They'll tell you that the old immigrant parish loyalties don't exist in the suburbs, despite patent evidence that many suburban parishes are even more tight-knit communities. If you try to tell them that the parish community is sacramental, a revelation of a peculiarly Catholic propensity for community formation rooted in the analogical imagination, they begin to babble about evangelization or empowering the poor or base communities in South America or how hard they work.

My late colleague Jim Coleman developed his theory of social capital—the resources that inhere in overlapping networks—from observation of the overlap of parochial, school, and parish networks in Catholic parishes. He noted that there were more resources available to the community than there would be if there were no such overlap. Somehow that never occurred to most parish priests and still doesn't. They may have heard of social capital, but they're just not interested.

Like all human institutions, the neighborhood parish has its built-in imperfections. Many parishes are very imperfect indeed, usually because of poor leadership. There are other institutions that also minister effectively to Catholics, campus chaplaincies, for example. However, one has to be blind not to perceive that when properly led by a personally secure, sensitive, and open pastor, neighborhood parishes generate levels of enthusiasm and commitment seldom matched in human history. The neighborhood/parish/school ought to be celebrated rather than taken for granted or ignored or, even worse, deplored.

How could the false prophets so quickly sweep away so much of the Catholic heritage? In the euphoria of the postconciliar years, as I have noted several times, a spirit of "anything goes" quickly became a spirit of "everything goes." The leaders of the Church—and here I mean the hierarchy—provided no wise and discerning leadership through the turbulent times of the 1960s and 1970s. Many of them strove to persuade people that nothing had changed or opposed all changes. In their absence the instant experts, the people who had read a book or attended a summer workshop or read the *National Catholic Reporter*, quickly filled the vacuum and justified their plans and programs with the same fervor and the same certainty that had characterized their support of the Sorrowful Mother novena not so long before. If there was not much depth to their response, little sense of history, a lack of good taste and good judgment, and virtually no consultation with the laity (who don't count anyway), then there was no one to dispute their vision or contest their victory.

To this day, they or their successors still seem to be in charge. The only opposition comes from those who want to turn back the clock completely, spin the altar around, put the Mass back in Latin, enshrine the tabernacle on the altar, and reimpose by law the Friday abstinence. Neither group seems to understand what it means to be a sacramental people.

I would like to be able to say that there exists a program for the recovery of the sacramental heritage in American Catholicism, a pedagogical literature about how to do it, syllabi for classroom instruction, national conferences at which ideas and projects are shared. Patently, nothing like this exists or is likely to exist at the present. The inertial energy of beige Catholicism continues unabated. I have to content myself at the end with the modest plea that someone should do something about it.

TWELVE

Religious Education and Beauty

The world in which we live needs beauty in order not to sink into despair. Beauty, like truth, brings joy to the human heart and is that precious fruit which resists the erosion of time.

Vatican II, cited by Pope John Paul II in his Easter letter to artists, "The Way of Beauty"

Liturgy should be enjoyable.

Pope John Paul II

The Church rejoices in human creativity and thanks God for the gift of artistic inspiration.

Cardinal Francis George

There comes a moment to everyone when beauty stands staring into the soul with sad, sweet eyes that sicken at the sound of words. And God help those who pass that moment by!

Edmund Rostand

Beauty will save the world!

Fyodor Dostoyevsky

I should note that this chapter is written from the perspective of "religion from below." I am not a theologian or a catechetical theorist. I am a sociologist, hence I must take a worm's-eye view of religious education and focus especially on the reactions of those we are trying to teach.

My thesis is that the beauty of the Catholic heritage, flawed as it often is in practice, especially in this country, attracts, enchants, and will not let people go no matter how hard they try to escape. To reshape this thesis, the question is not whether a Catholic catechesis can be beautiful but whether a catechesis that is not beautiful can possibly be Catholic. I do not suggest that we should abandon teaching doctrine. Catholics patently should know the doctrines of their religion. They should also experience the beauty in those doctrines.

Beauty, by way of brief introductory description, is a dimension of an object, event, or person that may, under proper circumstances, hint at the transcendent, otherness, *being*. Beauty on occasion provides an opportunity for the transcendent to break through briefly into our lives and illumine them. Beauty illuminates: it overcomes us with brilliant light. As Cardinal George has said, "Light, pure light seems to be the physical reality most often used to speak of God as beautiful." Thus to say that a wedding is beautiful (in this sense of the word) means that the love between the couple and the love for them of the priest and the community are so apparent and transparent that the dazzle of God's love transiently seems to fill the church, as it will be with them in their marriage bed for their first union as husband and wife. To say that a liturgy is beautiful means that the joy of the communal meal has so permeated the congregation that many sense that Jesus had indeed joined them at the table and is joyful with them. To say that a funeral ceremony (or whatever the liturgists call it these days) is beautiful is to say that the faith of the congregation in the triumph of life over death is so powerful that the Lord of the Resurrection seems temporarily to be among them, as he was with Lazarus' mourners, promising that life is too important ever to be anything but life. To say that a baptism is beautiful is to say that the celebration of priest and parents and godparents over this wondrous little bundle of human life is so delirious that they sense for a moment that the One who gives life and nurture is delirious with them. These moments, when well done, are exercises in the catechetics of beauty, the best advertisement, the best evangelization the Church could ever hope to have.

In American Catholicism today, beauty is mostly unimportant. Generally we begin with truth, usually of the propositional variety, beat it into the heads of our people so that they will be good (as we define good), and dispense with beauty, when we think about it at all, as an expensive option. Indeed, when pressed, we tend to say that beauty is a luxury and possibly a dangerous one because it interferes with goodness and may even lead to temptation. As proof, in a study of American congregations, my colleagues Peter Marsden and Mark Chaves discovered that Catholic parishes are least likely to provide artistic activities within the parish community or to recommend artistic performances or exhibitions beyond the parish boundaries (Chaves and Marsden 2000). If you're a Catholic parish, who needs beauty? Rules are important, epiphanies are not.

Someone has argued that one can judge the depth of a spirituality by the beauty of the art it produces. By that standard, contemporary American Catholic spirituality—nervous, frenetic, compulsive, always searching for new gimmicks—is worth very little.

The best contemporary Catholic theology agrees that of the three transcendentals inherent in Being—Truth, Goodness, and Beauty—the Beautiful is primary in that it is the one we encounter first. It overwhelms us, enchants us, fascinates us, calls us. As we ponder it, we see that it is good and we are attracted to the Goodness it represents. Finally, bemused by the appeal of goodness, we discover that it contains truth and we listen to the Truth we hear from it. This is not an inevitable process, nor one that involves logical deduction (though on our reflection after the experience we recognize a quasi logic). Rather, it is an existential tendency that seems to be built into the structure of the human condition.

There are, broadly speaking, two kinds of beauty—that which God has created and that which humans create in what may seem to many an almost blasphemous attempt to improve on God's work. We live surrounded by God's beauty. Sometimes we notice it. Sometimes, all too rarely perhaps, the beauty all around us invades us, stops us in our tracks, explodes within us—a stately cactus outlined against a rose gold sunset, the faint light of a winter sun on a smoothly frozen lake, the smell of mesquite in the air after a rainstorm, a goofy smile on a child's face as she tries her first brave steps, the touch of a friendly hand, the sun breaking through thick clouds after a storm, a well-proportioned human body, a meteor shower (or the aurora borealis) on a late summer night (tiger, tiger burning bright), an insect climbing the stalk of a plant, a chocolate malted milk with whipped cream, monarch butterflies flying along a beach on their way home. All are grace and grace is everywhere, often unnoticed, but still there.

Then why do we need human-created beauty? Why do we need human artists? The artist sees things more clearly than the rest of us. She penetrates into the illumination of being more intimately than do the rest of us. She wants us to see what she sees so that we can share in her illumination. She is driven to duplicate that beauty in her work. When van Gogh painted his golden fields he was endeavoring to share with us his instinctive vision of the fields and to make us see them more fully, more clearly, and more open to their illumination—as did filmmaker Akira Kurosawa when he had his tourist step into the world of van Gogh fields in his film *Colors*. The artist is a Sacrament maker, a creator of emphasized, clarified beauty designed to make us see, a person who invites us into the world she sees so that we can go forth from that world enchanted by the luminosity of her work and perhaps with enhanced awareness of the possibilities of life.

Is all created beauty implicitly religious? It is a complicated question on which art critics and theologians easily get hung up and which they are often unable to go beyond. For our purposes it suffices to say that much humanly created beauty that does not seem explicitly religious nonetheless is or can be religious, insofar as it tricks us into enchantment and thus opens us up to the illumination of being, stopping us in our tracks whether we want to be stopped in our tracks or not. The reconciliation arias at the end of the *Marriage of Figaro*, "New York Lights" in William Bolcom's *View from the Bridge*, American folk songs like "Shenandoah," a skyline viewed from a body of water in the moonlight, Roddy Doyle's *The Snapper*, Seamus Heany's love poem "The Otter," Rilke's protest that he needs no more springtimes because one is already too much for his blood, the joy of the drinking song in the first act of *Traviata* and, even more, Violetta becoming a

Christ figure, the hope that ugliness and terror cannot exorcise from a Stephen King novel, the much delayed triumph of good over evil in the fantasy saga of your choice, Molly Bloom's celebration of life and love in *Ulysses*. If grace is everywhere, it is superabundant in the world of art, when one is open to seeing it.

There are also works of beauty that abound that are explicitly religious though not presented in or produced under the auspices of a church: for example, such films as *Babette's Feast, All That Jazz, Always, Flatliners, Breaking the Waves, Dogma*. Paul Murray's poem that tells us that "he who needs nothing, he who brings all the gifts we give, needs us so that if we should cease to exist he would die of sadness." Graham Greene's *End of the Affair* and *The Power and the Glory*, Jon Hassler's *North of Hope*, Heaney's "We walk on air against our better judgement," the luminous ending of Alice McDermott's *Charming Billy*, the baptismal imagery in Bruce Springsteen's music, the passionate desire for redemption of their characters (creatures!) in the fiction of William Kennedy and David Lodge, the not quite inarticulate Mystery at the end of Brian Friel's later plays, the God who dances in *Dogma* as she does in the Book of Wisdom, the magic endings of the films of Eric Rohmer and Krzysztof Kieslowski.

Sometimes it is said that if God really wanted us to believe, he would speak to us. To which God might well reply that he shouts at us all the time through the beauty that surrounds us. We can hardly go anywhere without being inundated by beauty—except when we go to church. Even in church there is beauty in the Sacraments, but we seem determined to minimize the beauty so that we can emphasize the rules and regulations with which we have surrounded the Sacraments—in violation of canon law.

Not everyone will be stopped dead in his tracks and overcome by illumination (like St. Paul) by, for example, the pealing of the bells at the end of *Breaking the Waves,* by the Eucharistic image in *Babette's Feast,* by Ms. McDermott's narrator saying that it really doesn't make much difference for faith whether St. Philomena existed or not, by Molly Bloom, by "Shenandoah," by Heaney's resolutely non-ecclesiastical poetry, by Roy Scheider walking down the long tunnel to the fair spouse at the end of *All That Jazz.* There is no need for anyone to be entranced, enchanted, much less seduced by the beauty in these or any of the other examples I have given. My point rather is that grace is everywhere for those who are able to sense its presence and are generous in their search for it in what might seem strange places. We who try to teach religion should always be on the lookout for it and unafraid to absorb it for our own uses.

The experience of the beautiful can be depicted as an encounter with being that stops us in our tracks and illumines us. David Tracy describes the phenomenon of an encounter with a "classic" work of art (think of the Cathedral at Chartres): "When anyone of us is caught unawares by a genuine work of art, we find ourselves in the grip of an event, a happening, a disclosure, a claim to truth which we cannot deny and can only eliminate by our later controlled reflection." He adds, "We find ourselves caught up in its world. We are shocked, surprised, challenged by its startling beauty and its recognizable truth, its instinct for the essential. In the actual experience of art we do not experience the artist behind the work of art. Rather we recognize the truth of the work's disclosure of a world of reality transforming, if only for the moment, ourselves, our lives, our sense of possibilities, and actuality, our destiny."

Beauty is the strongest asset of Catholicism. When men and

women return to the Church after a long time of trying to "fall away," the most important thing for them is to be able to go to Mass again. The Sacraments are works of high beauty—the birth of a child, the consumption of a family meal, prayers at the bedside of the sick, the joining of the bodies and souls of two people in love, reconciliation after conflict. Small wonder that, even badly administered, they have a strong attraction for Catholics and are integral to the Catholic identity. Some will argue that it is not the purpose of the Sacraments to be beautiful but to dispense grace. Leaving aside the automatic, not to say superstitious, view of the Sacraments in that objection, one may simply reply that it is their very beauty that disposes them to dispense grace. They give grace efficiently because they are grace-full.

Closely attached to the Sacraments are the stories. All religions have stories. Religion is story before it's anything else and after it's everything else. Catholic stories are simply more beautiful— Christmas, Easter, Lent, May crownings, Holy Thursday processions and foot washing, First Communion, the Madonna and child, the saints, the angels, the souls in purgatory. Even when the stories are badly told—as they usually are—they are integral to the Catholic identity.

An observer of beauty says, "The link between the good and the beautiful stirs fruitful reflection. In a certain sense, beauty is the visible form of the good, just as the good is the metaphysical condition of beauty." This writer is talking to "all who are passionately dedicated to the search for new 'epiphanies' of beauty." Beauty and the art that creates it, in his perspective, become new "epiphanies" of God in the world. The writer is John Paul II in his Easter letter of 1999 to artists. The pope also said in his address that art is indispensable to the Church, a message that does not seem to have penetrated the frantic ideological posturing within American Catholicism. We are, with some happy exceptions, an "artless" Church, not because of Vatican II, but because we have no sense of the need for epiphanies, save those that are imposed on people by various projects of brainwashing and other forms of manipulation.

Beauty serves goodness and truth not by indoctrinating, not by educating, not by imparting doctrinally orthodox propositions. The beautiful illumines, it does not teach. Therefore, much of American Catholicism demands, what good does it do? Why bother with it?

There are two answers to this objection. The first is that nothing else produces instant effects, and the second is that the sense of enhanced awareness of the possibilities of life that beauty causes, sometimes in some people, does incline them in the direction of goodness. That's not enough for you? That's all you're going to get in this less than perfect world, and it's more than you're going to get by pounding obligations into their heads.

Artists have a creative intuition into what reality really is. It rises up from the depth of their personalities, a deep insight into the transcendent that illumines them. They are driven by the power of that illumination to share it with others, to make a sacrament, a beauty whose luminosity will enchant. They cannot, indeed they dare not, twist that creative intuition to fit other purposes, lest they destroy it. This is not because of the selfishness of the artist as creator of beauty. It is rather because the intuition of beauty, never completely under the artist's control, lays down its own conditions and demands respect under penalty of departing the scene. Thus Bernini's *Ecstasy of St. Theresa* flows from the intuition that erotic love is a metaphor for mystical ecstasy (an intuition he was not the first to discover). Had Bernini tried to tame that intuition so that it would not offend those who would be shocked by the metaphor, it would have been lost completely. Those who would tame the wild passion of creative intuition would deprive the sacrament maker of that which is essential to his vocation, an insight into being, into the really real. The appropriate response to art is patient generosity in which one opens oneself to the intuition that has driven the artist to create. It took me, for example, a whole week to absorb what William Kennedy was about in his *Ironweed*. If I had written of that brilliant work before the process of absorption was complete, I would have desecrated it.

Beauty, in other words, leads to truth in its own good time and in its own subtle way, and to truth that may not be perceived or expressed in precisely the terms that the eager religion teacher would want. Beauty by its very nature inclines us to both truth and goodness, but only when one is willing to respect the subtle dynamics of this inclination—and to accept that the process is not by any means automatic.

Father Richard Viladesau writes:

> Art is an effective moral educator in that it portrays vice and virtue rather than legislating about them or explaining them in theoretical terms. Narrative art is particularly apt at teaching about human fallibility. The fundamental moral evil of "seeing the worse for the better," for example, is more informatively (though of course less systematically) carried out by poets, playwrights, and novelists than by moral philosophers and theologians. Likewise, virtue is more convincing and imitable when it is embodied concretely in art than when it is commanded or expounded theoretically. Perhaps in gen-

eral art proves more than philosophy can. Art need not be didactic in order to serve the good—although there is clearly also a place for beauty and art in preaching and teaching, as in every form of communication. Art as communication can have a transformative effect on the person because it can literally give us a new way of seeing, hearing, feeling. (Viladesau 1999)

Art is, or can be, an epiphany at work.

Thus the magic ending of Rohmer's *My Night at Maud's*, with its dramatic shift from the hill over Clermont to the Riviera beach, is surely an epiphany about intense human love, just as Kieslowski's *Blue* is an epiphany about letting go of grief. However, it requires time to absorb those epiphanies, to make them part of our soul. Some people will never be able to absorb them. Even those who finally "get it" will not necessarily change their attitudes or behavior because of such epiphanies.

Our heritage is not a series of doctrinal propositions or moral imperatives. It is primarily a story of God's implacably forgiving love. Religion does not speak in abstract concepts, religion speaks in stories, in the language of images. Human knowledge is primarily the knowledge of story. We tell one another stories to explain ourselves and the world in which we live. Story, the understanding of one event through a similar event, according to some scholars, came into our evolutionary development even before language and made language both possible and necessary. Story—narrative metaphor—tells us that something is like something else. Because we are reflective as well as narrating animals, we must reflect on our stories and derive rational and propositional formulations from them. Religion is primarily a story of grace. Doctrinal and moral codes are derivatives from that story, necessary derivatives indeed, but still derivatives. When we separate them from the story of grace, they lose their raw energy and power. Beauty is, in the final analysis, grace intervening spectacularly in our lives to enhance and confirm our existing stories of grace. Or, to look at it from a metaphysical viewpoint, Beauty is Being breaking through to assure us of Its benignity. Or, to put it religiously, beauty is the Holy Spirit dancing through the universe like a cosmic Tinkerbell, sparking off from Her magic wand countless signs of the presence of grace, a presence that we are likely to encounter anywhere and everywhere, save in a church or various obligatory religious instruction classes.

Patently, I am not saying that the formal catechism—in whatever form—should be abandoned. It is still important. I am rather saying that we should attend also to beauty—a small tear in the surface of the world, according to Simone Weil, that pulls us through to some vaster space. Beauty lifts us off the ground, spins us around, and then deposits us back on the ground, perhaps only a few inches away. It is not that we no longer stand at the center of the world—we never did. We no longer stand at the center even of our own world. Rather, we are still in the power of that which has happened to us in our encounter with beauty. It is the ethical alchemy of beauty.

Such events don't always happen, and when they do they do not necessarily transform behavior in the way that a weekend "encounter" of whatever kind is supposed to transform behavior (and does not and cannot, because we are far too complex creatures to be brainwashed in such a short period of time). However, encounters of beauty do open us up to their own alchemy, which gently guides us to goodness and truth. There is simply no other way, because faith and ethics cannot be imposed from the outside.

They can be embraced only as a consequence of an act of love. We continue to teach the catechism with the modest realization that our efforts will be effective only when grace intervenes, when the Spirit touches the pupil with His magic wand. We don't push, we don't threaten, we don't force compliance.

Beauty is created by artists, natural beauty by the divine artists, humanly constructed beauty by the human artist. The pope tells us that "the divine artist passes on to the human artist a spark of his own surpassing wisdom, calling him to share in his creative power." If you don't have artists or if you don't want to have them hanging around, you won't have beauty. I include among artists not only the painters, sculptors, poets, architects, musicians, and writers who do what is considered art (fine as well as lively) but also folk artists and personal artists and family artists. The pope begins his address to artists by telling them that artists are metaphors for God. God creates the great Sacrament of the universe to respond to His conception of the universe, the artist creates her own sacrament of beauty in response to the artistic insight that has captured her imagination and to the service of which she dedicates her skills. The pope also insists that those who feel this divine spark must "put it at the service of their neighbor and humanity as a whole."

American Catholicism does not much care for artists. They tend to be a little odd and not to understand the need to indoctrinate the Catholic laity by art that drives home important doctrinal points. They also want to be paid for their work, sometimes demanding exorbitant prices. It is much easier to work with "artists" who do what they are told and do it cheaply. Is their work beautiful? Who cares!

The fundamental purpose of education is to prepare the student for beauty. The purpose of Catholic education, among other things, is to help the student be open to the Spirit as He manifests Himself in the beautiful. That may be a hard saying. How does one go about doing that? Where are the textbooks, the syllabi, the visual aides that can enable us to do that? I have no answers to those questions. I merely note that the religious and moral metanoia are likely to occur only under the impulse of a person's being stopped in his tracks and then drenched in luminosity by an encounter with beauty.

Won't too much concern for beauty turn people into sensualists? Won't their passions be aroused by beauty? Won't they get dirty thoughts? Humans, being bodily creatures, are by definition sensualists. If God had thought that human sensations were evil, he should not have given us bodies. Grace enters our personalities through bodily experiences. The Sacraments are sensual experiences, including especially matrimony, in which bodies are, as it were, freely exchanged for the purpose of pleasure and love. Doubtless some of those who pursue beauty do so for pleasure and nothing else. But there is no human activity that is without danger of distortion and abuse. Sense experiences usually do not produce dedicated sensualists who lie on their chaises in the sunshine, eating bonbons and listening to Mozart.

What can be done to introduce beauty into the life of American Catholicism? Into its education? Into its schools? Into its religious instruction? Into the administration of the Sacraments? Into its liturgy?

The perspective that sees no need for Beauty has been around a long time. It will not die gracefully. I cannot outline a program for the restoration of beauty that one could take home and implement. There are, however, some suggestions that might help, over the long term, to promote the apologetics of beauty:

1. Be quiet and listen. This is a hard saying for our clergy and quasi clergy. Having all the answers and being compelled to impose these answers, the clerisy sees no need and certainly has no time for listening. No one is listening to the laypeople on the subject, because everyone knows what the laypeople should hear. If we did stop to listen to the laity, really listen, we would find how deeply (albeit not perfectly) spiritual they really are. It would have been wise to have dedicated the Great Jubilee Year to asking the laity to evangelize us. That will be the year, won't it, when we are willing to risk the possibility that the laity are better Catholics than we are!

A pastor I know has the practice of asking his eighth graders to write him a brief letter in which they tell him why they want to receive confirmation. It is not a condition for the Sacrament but an attempt to discover what goes on in the spiritual lives of these early teens. Each year he is astonished by the religious depth these young people reveal in their letters and their subsequent ten-minute discussions with him.

Only if we really listen to the laity and resist the impulse to impose our corrections and clarifications on what they say will we begin to realize that we do them an enormous injustice. They are far better Catholics than we are willing to admit and far better Catholics than many of us are—even if they don't always use "correct" language in talking about their graces and their spiritual needs.

2. Abandon compulsion. Urge the laity to attend classes as preparation for the Sacraments, but do not force them to do so.

The advantage of this strategy is that it compels us to make these classes truly excellent, the sort of experience of which people will say afterward, "That was really great! It was a wonderful experience! Am I glad I did it." Only when that sort of image of our sacramental classes seeps into the parish will people come willingly and eagerly. Such classes should celebrate the joy and the beauty of the Sacrament. As Bishop John McCarthy has said, when you open the door of the rectory to someone seeking a Sacrament, ask yourself how the Good Shepherd would greet them. Or, I add, Mary the Mother of Jesus and Our Mother. Neither one, incidentally, would revel in the power of being able to deny a Sacrament.

I know of a priest who, when someone calls about a baptism, asks the parents to bring the kid over to the rectory because he'd like to meet him. What a wonderful child, he says excitedly. How God must love this perfect little being. He asks them some questions about how their family life is going and praises their generosity and subtly offers help if they are having troubles. If it is the first child, he asks how they met and when they first knew they were in love. Ten, fifteen minutes at the most.

3. Make the administration of the Sacrament an experience of joy and of such luminous beauty that even the most hardened, "fallen away" Catholic will be tempted to return soon. The joy must be real, not the cutesy kind of joy in which we announce that now we're all going to be joyous. Obviously the minister of the Sacrament must truly enjoy what he is doing, he must love the babies he is baptizing, the couples at whose marriage he is presiding, the kids receiving their First Communion or confirmation. He should dote over each wondrous baby and celebrate his or her arrival. The babies are, after all, our future, indeed our future

parishioners. Thank God they're here! At last! What wonderful little tykes! Baptism should be a high for the minister (even if he misses a quarter of a football game!), one of the high points of his week. (If there are siblings present, they might be brought into the act—asked whether they think we ought to baptize the baby, invited to touch the baby's forehead as we welcome this new Catholic into the Church, quizzed about whether they think the baby will cry. You can't go wrong if you're nice to the little ones, even if they are sometimes inclined to run around the Church while you're continuing with the Sacrament!)

How can the presiding priest not be filled with awe at the mystery of human passion that brings a young woman and a young man together to join body and soul in marriage. Even if they seem to be nerds, more interested in getting a hall than in the marriage ceremony, they still are brave and courageous young people, taking a huge risk with their lives. The presider should admire them and make patent his admiration and his pleasure in sharing their joy. Should he not in his own way love them as much as, if not more than, their families, because they too are the future of our heritage?[1]

The pope ended his address to artists with a quote from Prince Myshkin in Dostoyevsky's *The Idiot*: "Beauty will save the world!" Many American Catholics would ask, How is beauty going to raise concern for the environment, for the poor, for racial justice, for the right to life, for gender equality? How indeed.

In his 1970 Nobel Prize speech, Aleksandr Solzhenitsyn reflected on Prince Myshkin's idiocy:

> "Beauty will save the world." What does this mean? For a long time it seemed to me that it was merely a phrase. How

could such a thing be possible? When in our bloodthirsty history did beauty ever save anyone, and from what? It has ennobled, elevated, yes; but who has it saved?

Only there is something so peculiar at the core of beauty, a peculiarity in the position of art: the conviction carried by a genuine work of art is absolute and conquers even a resisting heart. A work of art contains its verification in itself. Artificial, strained concepts do not withstand the test of being turned into images; both concepts and images fall to pieces, they show themselves to be sickly and pale, they convince no one. But works which draw on truth and present it to us concentrated and alive seize us, powerfully join us to themselves and no one ever, even centuries from now, will come forth to refute them.

Then perhaps the old tri-unity of Truth, Goodness, and Beauty is not simply a showy, worn-out formula as we thought in the time of our self-confident, materialistic youth? If the tops of these three trees meet, as scholars have declared, but the too obvious, too straight sprouts of Truth and Goodness have been knocked down, cut off, and do not grow—then perhaps the capricious, unpredictable, unexpected sprouts of Beauty will force their way through and rise to that very same place, and thus carry out the work for all three?

And then it is not a mistake, but a prophecy that we find written in Dostoyevsky: "Beauty *will* save the world."

So says Dostoyevsky, so says Solzhenitsyn, so says John Paul II. And what then do we say?

THIRTEEN

Authority as Charm

A young village girl told me that, when I am about to talk to anyone, I picture Jesus Christ and how gracious and friendly he was to everyone.

John Vianney

The fear of beauty is rooted under the roots of fear.

Marie Ponsot

In this chapter I propose that the problem of authority is experienced in the Church not so much with the authority exercised by the Vatican or by the Chancery Offices but by the local parish.[1] For weal or woe, the laity figure that the former two levels are far away, have no direct influence on their lives, and can safely be ignored. However, it is in the local parish where the Church exercises its only remaining power to control the lives of the people— the denial of access to the Sacraments. Reception of baptism, confirmation, First Communion, and matrimony has often been turned into an obstacle course the laity must survive, rather than experiences of grace. Many of them come away from the experience not transformed by an encounter with grace but bitterly angry at the Church.

I propose to suggest a reform of authority at this local level and then argue that a similar reform should occur up the line. Relying on the theology of John Shea and the scriptural analysis of Roland Murphy, O. Carm., I propose that the Church remodel its authority to reflect God more as final cause than as efficient cause, God as inviting, calling, attracting instead of God as controlling, directing, regulating, God as Omega more than Alpha, God as the one who gathers in the fragments more than God of the Big Bang. To change the quasi-philosophical terminology by turning to the three transcendentals, the Church should put more emphasis on the Beautiful in its exercise of authority. As theologian Hans Urs von Balthasar says, we apprehend first the Beautiful and perceive that it is Good and then finally that it is True. Often, it seems, in contemporary American Catholicism, we start with the True and never get beyond it.

At the parish level this would mean that the relevant authority figures—directors of music, liturgy, religious education, and RCIA—would see their authority mission as to invite, charm, and enchant the laity as they approach the Sacraments, instead of imposing rules and regulations, creating obstacles, and demanding compliance. Their job would not be to say, "This is what you have to do before you (or your child) can have the Sacrament," but instead, "These are the resources we can make available to you as you prepare for the Sacrament." Preparation for and reception of a Sacrament should then become a rich and glorious celebration of the presence of Grace, a presence that would be reflected in the gracefulness of the parish staff. If the members of the class have to take the course, the instructor doesn't have to worry about the Beauty of God, the Church, and the Sacrament. Similarly, as I argued in the previous chapter, the sacramental ritual itself should be elegant, moving, joyous, memorable, the kind of experience of which one can honestly say, "It was so beautiful I will never forget it."

This is not easily done. It requires training, time, intelligence, and money. I doubt that most parish staffs are capable of it. Moreover, many parish staff members, including, it is to be feared, priests, see such an approach as optional—fine if you have the time and money but not really important or necessary. They misunderstand the role of Beauty in sacramentality as reflecting God's beauty.

The laypeople, they will tell you (often with their eyes glowing with zeal), don't understand what Catholicism is and they do not live Catholic lives. They are secularists, consumerists, materialists. They must be converted. Preparations for the Sacraments are one of the few times that we have to teach them about Christianity and the Church and change the direction of their lives. Pre-Sacrament classes are something like retreats in which we aim for conversion. If there's no sign of conversion we can't let them receive the Sacraments. Only Catholics can receive the Sacraments and these people aren't really Catholic. Reactions such as these suggest that parish staffs have succumbed to the terrible temptation to do good, that is, to impose virtue by force.

Their assumptions about the religious faith of the laity are gratuitous, demeaning, patronizing—and contradicted both by the empirical data and by open-minded anecdotal contact with the laity. Moreover, canon law guarantees that the laypeople have the right to receive the Sacraments, a right that can be denied only on rare occasions. The addition of requirements is a violation of canon law. One cannot even demand a pre-Cana conference as a condition for the reception of the Sacrament of matrimony. One can strongly urge participation in preparatory classes, after one has made sure that they will be well done, but one cannot insist.

Furthermore, as St. Thomas has insisted, virtue is a habit acquired by the repetition of free acts. Actions that are compelled do not develop virtue. Obstacle courses don't work. It is psychologically naïve (and patently so) to assume that six classes or twelve classes or even two years of RCIA will induce fundamental changes in human behavior. In the short run, brainwashing (and compulsory classes are a form of usually inefficient brainwashing) may produce superficial effects. Long-term impact, however, has to come from a change in religious environment, an exposure to the Beauty of sacramental liturgy (which is also difficult and expensive), and through that liturgy to a God who calls, who gathers together the fragments. There is no way such a long-term environment can be created in a couple of weeks.

Often, that which is done in the name of making people better Catholics in fact alienates them from the Church. It is no longer possible (indeed it has never been possible) to force men and women to become better Catholics. There is no alternative (and there never has been) to a strategy of attracting them with Beauty. To the extent that people remain Catholic, the reason is because they are caught up in the beauty of sacramental Catholicism and the stories it tells, no matter how shoddy the presentation of beauty is or how inept the telling of stories. Beauty and the charm it exercises on the human personality are not options. Without them we fail. Strategically, perhaps more than ever (though only perhaps), we will communicate the Good and the True only (or mostly, if one wishes) through the Beautiful.

Why then do members of parish teams try to control rather than attract, dominate rather than invite, force rather than charm, push rather than call? Perhaps some of them are not very charming people and would find such an orientation difficult. However, what reason do they have to think that Church authority ought to be charming, that it ought to reflect the God that calls? Most of the examples they see of the exercise of Church authority are innocent of charm. To possess some of the Church's authority is a license to control, not an invitation to invite, not a mandate to call. How else do you act in the name of the Church except by controlling people's lives? Isn't that what hierarchy is for? Why do we have to be charming parish staff when pastors and bishops and Vatican officials are not charming?

I wonder often whether parish staff members and priests ought to have a course from the people who administer the Four Seasons hotel chain on how to be friendly and attractive to the people they welcome to the Sacraments. As it is now, it often seems as if they have been trained by the U.S. Postal Service.

Thus I come to my main argument: There must be a reform, at every level in the Church, in which authority moves in the direction of charm, of the final cause, of the Beauty of an incredibly attractive God, of a God who calls, even of a God who tries to lure with Beauty. I do not say that all activities which might be subsumed under the rubric of efficient cause (the philosophical term is used loosely here) should be abandoned. Any community needs bookkeeping and housekeeping rules, decision-making executives, and institutions which protect the rights and freedom of its members. Someone has to stop parish staff from abusing the rights of the laity. Someone has to protect people from sexual abuse. Someone has to launch fund-raising drives. Someone has to oversee the training of parish staff both lay and clerical. The change I propose is less drastic and (perhaps) more subtle. At every level of the Church leaders and teachers should realize that Beauty (by which Goodness and Truth are most attractively presented) is their strongest tool, and today, perhaps especially, the only really effective weapon for drawing the faithful closer to the Church and to the God for which the Church is a sacrament. They must understand that it will not do to appeal and invite until it does not work and then fall back on control. Rather, they must persist in attraction as their only effective long-run strategy. Obviously such a shift will be wrenching. I would suggest that there isn't much choice.

Jesus was the most charming man who ever lived. People followed him because of his enormous attractiveness and the appeal of the good news he preached. (Why does the word "evangelization" on the mouths of many clerics seem so unattractive? Why does it sound so often like high-powered advertising mixed with enthusiastic brainwashing?) Jesus was, in full theological literalness, the embodiment of the God who called.

Christianity spread through its early years because it was so attractive. Professor Rodney Stark has persuasively argued that Constantine's establishment of Christianity was a shrewd acceptance of an accomplished fact: Christianity was well on its way to becoming the religion of most people in the Roman Empire. Professor Stark (who claims he is not a Christian, or at least not a practicing one) says that the appeal of the new religion was that Christians were such good people, good indeed to their relatives and friends, but good to everyone. "By this all shall know that you are my disciples . . . "

Active control of the lives of the faithful (to the extent that it was possible) came as part of the conversion of the barbarians, as the Church sought to Christianize those who had been converted en masse and sometimes by the sword. Even then, Alcuin argued with Charlemagne that conversion of the Saxons by force was wrong. Moreover, wherever the Irish monks prevailed there were never any forced conversions. Rather, the Irish established monasteries and monastery schools and attracted by their charm the local pagan nobility. (Whether charm is a virtue in the Irish or merely a genetically programmed trait need not detain us here.) Nonetheless, for centuries, as the Church strove to Christianize the so-called barbarians, it normally felt the need to force virtue upon them. Ironically, it was probably the beauty and the stories of Christianity that most impressed the poorly educated laity and their poorly educated clergy.

Authoritative control no longer works anywhere, not even in Northern European and the North American countries (Germany, the Netherlands, Britain, Ireland, Canada, the United States—and by extension Australia and New Zealand). In the destabilization of nineteenth-century Catholic structures that resulted from the reforms of the Second Vatican Council, Church hierarchy lost all remaining ability to force the consent of its members. There is no longer a secular arm, no longer even the threat of mortal sin. Men and women are Catholic on their own terms. This situation may be good or not, but it is real. Attempts to restore the docile (and it wasn't always so docile) obedience of the first half of the previous century cannot work, because such attempts assume that the laity still concede to authority the right to demand that obedience. In fact, the confidence in and credibility of Church authority is declining rapidly in both North Atlantic and Eastern European countries. What is left of the Church's power to control? The Church can deny Sacraments to the laity and violate its own laws, but in that case the faithful will often shop for another parish where they can receive the Sacraments. It can warn them that they are committing mortal sins, but the laity all over the world have reserved to themselves the right to decide what is mortal sin and what isn't. Because of the priest shortage, bishops are reluctant to crack down on pastors. The Vatican can denounce a theologian, but unless he is a priest there's no way to stop him from engaging in objectionable behavior. If the objectionable theologian is lay, he can perhaps be barred from Catholic universities. But the Church has no power to do anything to a lay theologian teaching at a secular university. Control is finished. Hierarchy has no choice but to fall back on the appeal of Beauty.

The primary role of hierarchy, it is said, is to protect the faith. Might not its primary role instead be to present the faith in all its attractiveness and thereby protect it in the most effective way possible? Investigations and condemnations may still be necessary, but they don't have much impact and should only be a means of last resort.[2]

Those with authority, it is said, have the right to demand obedience from those under their authority. Granted for the sake of the argument that there is such a right, it seems unlikely that it can be effectively exercised (at any time or place in history) in the absence of effective sanctions. The Vatican can sanction bishops and priests, and bishops can sanction priests. But there are no sanctions available that can be applied to the laity. It is unlikely, therefore, that this right, should it exist, can be effectively exercised.

Finally, it may be argued, a pastor, a priest, a pope should be the efficacious sign of unity in his community and therefore must strive to control, direct, and regulate, lest unity be lost. Calling, inviting, charming are luxuries he cannot afford. I would argue that a hierarch's most effective strategy for becoming a sign of unity is precisely to stand as a Sacrament of a Church that calls and a God who calls.

Let us consider the issue on the parish level by studying two pastors. Pastor Primus believes in a well-regulated parish, so he has rules for everything. Because it is proper liturgically, for example, he insists that bride and groom must march down the aisle together instead of meeting at the front. At a wedding rehearsal he lays down all the rules that must be followed in his parish. Several times during a wedding or funeral liturgy he warns that those who are not Catholic may not receive Communion. He is stern with the grammar school kids, who, he believes, must be taught respect and discipline. He bans teenagers from the parish gym because they are destructive. He insists that he need not follow any recommendations of the parish council, the school board, or the finance committee because they are only advisory. He does not consult on Mass schedules. Parish liturgy is poor because he does not believe in wasting a lot of money on an organist. His homilies are long and boring. He insists on absolute obedience from the parish staff. He rarely smiles and is nervous and defensive with laywomen who, he believes, want to take over the Church. He argues that his tough approach to authority in the parish is necessary to preserve unity.

Pastor Secundus works for consensus and cooperation. He has his own ideas about what needs to be done in the parish but he listens, persuades, argues, and even changes his mind. Rarely does he say a flat "no." He is a polished preacher and supports an extensive liturgy program. The kids claim that he is a good friend. The teens adore him. He listens, listens, listens. He likes and respects women. He is always open to new ideas. The various factions and groups in the parish are convinced he understands their problems and perspectives. Like a good precinct captain, he tries to keep everyone happy and usually does. At wedding rehearsals, he turns to the bride (and the bride's mother) and asks, "How do you folks want to do this?" When faced with difficulties, his first words are "Let's see how we can work this out." He seems a genuinely happy, secure, and joyous man who likes being a parish priest and likes people. Occasionally he will whisper to someone who thinks he ought to be tougher, "Ah sure, don't you catch more flies with honey?"

Which pastor is a more efficacious sign of unity in his parish? Cannot the themes latent in this typology be applied up the hierarchical line, even to the very top?

The multi-volume history of the Vatican Council by Guiseppe Alberigo and Joseph Komonchak describes the resistance of the curial opponents to the convening of the Council as having been based on the fear that the Church ought not to trust the bishops of the world, and the theologians and the laity, because all were infected by the evil doctrines that permeate the modern world—even though the bishops were men of the Curia's own choosing.

If the old mechanisms of control were abandoned, the Church would be overwhelmed. For weal or woe, however, the old methods of control were destabilized by the Council and no longer operate and will never operate again. Control is finished. There seems no alternative to charm that reveals Charm.

FOURTEEN

Liturgists and the Laity

In the coupling of these sacred callings and network effects, liturgists such as Bob have difficulty taking the role of others involved in parish work. Liturgists find their intolerance a virtue, their unveiling of others' liturgical ignorance as educational, their politics as righteous, their disdain as caring, and their failures as successes. These are the ironic experiences that rest inside the situation of the oppositional insider, and they are the experiences that fuel the terrorism inflicted by liturgists in the name of holier worship practices. What is clear about Bob's trajectory is that the existing moral orders of parish life that confront him as he enters each parish are of little importance to him other than as a set of arrangements that must be radically changed.

Michael J. McCallion and David R. Maines

I always tell the staff here that, if people do not come to church, we have to ask ourselves first "Why?" instead of first blaming people for not looking at the world as church ministers do. I tell them that if we have nothing compelling enough to cause people to attend, then we have failed Jesus—the people have not failed.

Monsignor Ignotus

It is symptomatic of the problems of liturgy and liturgists that there has never been a national survey of the impact on the laity and the reaction of the laity to liturgical reform. One can only conclude that the laity don't count, so they don't get to vote. Much less do liturgists feel they need to learn in any systematic way about the laity's experience of the liturgy. Have not such liturgical prophets as Aidan Kavanagh and Richard Galliardetz written of the laity as middle class, suburban, consumerist materialists? Who cares what they think?

Liturgists tend to be apriorists—and not infrequently, elitist apriorists. They have the truth, learned in workshops, study days, national conferences, and graduate school programs (or like the Bob described in the epigraph, "a couple of courses at the seminary"). It is their role to impose this truth on the laity, however reluctant the laity may be to accept it. According to Professor Frederic Roberts's gentle description of their attitudes in the Spring 1995 issue of *Liturgy Digest*, liturgists insist that a firm line must be drawn between themselves and those who disagree with them, and indeed between themselves and those dissidents within their number who wander from true belief. The difference between these folks and those who ran Catholic schools before 1960 escapes me. Both groups are authoritarian (though liturgists and their cousins may think they are liberals), both groups want to force virtue, though for the good of those being forced, and both groups are immune to compromise.

Liturgists are, to use a sociological term, a sect within the Church, and often an arrogant and authoritarian sect at that.

I must confess that I am an empiricist, perhaps even a radical empiricist. My empiricism is instinctive and antedates and probably caused my obsession with sociological data. When I enter a situation (a parish, a community, a university), I poke around, listen, and try to sniff out the relational patterns, the influence networks, the convictions and the dislikes of my colleagues. I am less interested for the moment in what they ought to be than in what they are. I want to know about my colleagues' fears, their hopes, their expectations. Perhaps I will learn something from them. I might even grow to like them, though I may disagree with them on many things. No, I will certainly grow to like most of them and to sympathize with them.

I don't do this all the time, for which God forgive me, and I never do it as well as I should. Nor is it virtue on my part to engage in this ongoing reconnaissance. It's programmed in my bones, in my genes, in my culture, in my upbringing. I am doomed forever to be a precinct captain, to want to know the neighborhood.

It is my impression that liturgists (with their cousins hereinafter always included) would think this odd behavior, indeed would be wary of it. While it is good to know one's people, one has not come to negotiate with them but to convert them. One has not come to listen to them, but to teach them truth about worship. One is among them to evangelize them, or, more properly, to reevangelize them. What do they know about worship anyway?

Right?

Might not the liturgist who has been seduced by radical empiricism be willing to tolerate those who mumble the rosary in the back of church or light votive candles or refuse to hold hands at the Lord's Prayer or ignore the exchange of peace or keep their mouths firmly shut at hymn time? Might he not willingly grant their freedom to dissent from his party line? Might he not limit his efforts to persuasion and charm and never denounce or order?

What kind of liturgist would that be?

It is at this raw, gut level of preconscious orientation that I find myself in disagreement with and often deeply offended by liturgists (there are of course many happy exceptions). I am affronted by their constant desire to create new symbols (as though Catholicism didn't already have a rain forest of symbols), which are often cute, artsy, and empty—when they don't offend the laity (like draining holy water fonts at the beginning of Lent or insisting that ministers of the Eucharist receive last instead of first). I am angered when they destroy brilliant rituals for their own ideological purposes—as the RCIA people have strangled the Easter Vigil by extending its length to three and a half, even four hours, thus driving away most of the parish. I want to scream when I see liturgists pushing kids around so they will get in proper procession lines. I am furious when they tell me that for a church to be liturgically correct it must be almost as bare as a Benedictine chapel. I want to cry out in pain when they forbid second-grade May crownings in Catholic schools.

At no point have they consulted about any of these things with the Catholic laity. What do they know? Does the Holy Spirit permeate them? How dare one suggest that the Spirit might be at work among the suburban middle class?

When Father Kavanagh and his ilk tell me how bad the suburban middle class is, I grow furious. These are my people. In my experience (and in my data), they are more generous, more faithful, and more dedicated than many if not most of us in the clerical caste (including liturgists). Many in the clerical caste have no trouble generating sympathy and compassion for the peoples of the "Third World"—with whom they don't work—but have only contempt for their own people, who for some reason have no call on either sympathy or compassion.

There is, then, little ground for dialogue between me and the liturgists. We differ not merely on first principles but also in gut instincts. They see no need for research on the reaction of the laity to liturgical reform. I believe that in the absence of such research, liturgists will continue to stumble around in darkened halls. Thirty-five years after the end of the Vatican Council, only 18 percent of Catholic laity rate their clergy as "excellent" on preaching (less than half the proportion of Protestants who assign an "excellent" score to their clergy). Only a quarter rate worship as "excellent." All the fussbudgeting of the liturgists hasn't accomplished very much.

Catholics like the Eucharist. In addition, as I noted in an earlier chapter, there is a correlation between frequency of Church attendance and participation in the fine arts. Even if it is badly done, as it usually is, the liturgy has an impact on people. They simply ignore the empty holy water fonts and the other gimmickry. Yet they will also tell you that the Mass in its present form is "boring!" Some liturgists will respond by saying that the Eucharist is the worship of God, and that true Christians (as opposed to suburban bourgeoisie) would never find it boring. However, the pope himself has said that the liturgy should be entertaining.

At a higher level, "official" liturgists, scholars, experts, theologians, and bishops (none of whom have any more of a clue than do the ordinary parish liturgists) will pontificate on what must be changed to make the liturgical effort better. Almost always their recommendations involve more of the same—change things to restore the old solemn spirit of the liturgy (have they forgotten how bad it was in the1950s?), bring the tabernacle back into the church, keep the priest on the altar separated from the people, make the Eucharist more solemn, restore the sweep of the old Roman "collects," et cetera, et cetera.

On both sides of the great (and, as it seems to me, foolish) debate about the reform of Paul VI, the discussion is dominated by neo-rubricists—people concerned about when the congregation sits or stands or kneels, who does what and when and where, what kind of vestments are worn, what the priest may do, what the deacon may do, what the people may do, what everyone must do. Almost from the beginning of postconciliar liturgical reform, many liturgists seemed to be converted rubricists, insisting on the punctilious enforcement of precise rules. Foolishly I thought that we had left all that behind. However, rubrical nitpickers are alive and well and dominate the liturgy.

None of these neo-rubrical changes, however meritorious, will make any difference at all. The laity might be horrified if the priest turns his back on them again, they might be affronted if he does not come down into the church to exchange peace with them, they might love to hear chant and polyphony again, they might be delighted if the priest no longer plays cute little games with the text of the canon. They might be pleased if the tedious Prayers over the Faithful are shortened, freed from ideology, or maybe even eliminated. They might be delighted if semiliterate lectors were all shot at sunrise.

None of these changes or any of the others proposed in this open season on the reform of Paul VI will make the Eucharist any less boring than it is. Cardinal Ratzinger deplores the reform, but what does he know about its effect in the parishes? Like everyone else in the business, liturgy for him is an a priori game from which the laity have been excluded.

One should know not only the lay reaction to all the abrupt fads and fashions that sweep through the liturgical market place; one should also know the needs, the expectations, the hopes, the fears of the laity to which the liturgical event might address itself. Can there be a meeting between historical and theological notions of worship and the people's worship needs?

In all candor I must say I doubt it, not as long as liturgists (high and low) imagine themselves as a persecuted minority and act like a religious sect. Liturgists listen, whether in the parish or the chancery or the Vatican? Why should they listen when no one else in the Church is listening?

The problem is deeper than abominable homilies or the fussing of the neo-rubricists or the zany experiments of the lunatic left. The problem of liturgists is fundamental in the ministry of the Church today and affects all forms of Catholic ministry, formation, and education. It is the gratuitous assumption that the Catholic laity are not really Catholic and need to be reconverted, reevangelized, reeducated, redone. Father Kavanagh's jeremiads are only an exaggerated version of this assumption. Proof? As a bishop said to me, "They don't do what we tell them to do."

That about says it.

So we issue new catechisms that explain at the length of a thirteenth-century tractate what they really have to believe, we institute parish workshops to "renew" them, we run year-long reevangelization campaigns to lead them back to the faith, we shape our liturgy programs to constrain them to worship correctly, and we force them into educational rituals when they want their children to be baptized or even when they are asked to be sponsors at baptism and confirmation. They go along with this nonsense because they like being Catholic and because they have learned through the years that if you're Catholic you have to endure certain pointless or even foolish exercises in jumping through hoops.

My quite modest suggestion (well, it's really revolutionary) is that we consider the possibility that the laity on the average are men and women of solid faith, perhaps more solid than ours, that we can learn much from their faith, perhaps more than they can learn from us, and that our mission is not to redo them but rather to assist them (with respect) to develop an even richer and deeper faith than they already have. (As for the protest that they don't do what we tell them to do, I can only say forget about it fellows, we lost that control over their lives long ago and we'll never get it back!) That they are that kind of people is proven by the fact that after thirty-five traumatic and crazy years they're still in the Church, that most of them show no signs of leaving, and that our worst idiocies have not driven them out.

I observe how they cope with marital tension, child rearing, teenage conflict, career discouragement, disappointment, sickness, failing parents, fatal illness, and death, how they tolerate incompetent priests and unspeakably bad homilies, how when given half a chance they convert their parishes into centers of dedication and charity the like of which have rarely been seen in the history of Christianity. I note with interest their continued generosity with their money and their time (even though they alone of American religionists have no say about how the money is spent), and how eagerly they contribute to the annual missionary appeal and how charitable they are in response to requests for voluntary service.

All right, they have limitations—unlike priests and religious educators and RCIA directors and parish liturgists. Nonetheless, it seems to me to be obvious that on average, they are good people who do not deserve to be hassled or harried or harassed or denounced or processed through experiences that will remake them.

We are, in fact, pretty darn lucky that they're still around.

Liturgy, above all else, should be warm, encouraging, hopeful. It should provide a congregation with the boost, the jump start that will sustain its members through the difficulties, the worries, the strains of the week ahead. I see no reason there cannot be challenge in such a liturgy too, but a challenge mixed in with encouragement, warmth, and hope.

"Do you know how hard I work?" priests ask me. The proper answer is that you probably don't work as hard as your laymen and -women do. For most people in our parishes, most of the time, the crises and demands of family relationships, mixed with aging and the approach of death, are the biggest challenges of their lives. I fail to find in most of what I read any awareness in the Church's leaders and parish programmers of the anguish (and the ecstasy) of these challenges. One could go through a whole liturgical year in many parishes and not hear a word that would suggest that the Church is aware of such strains in the lives of its people.

Would it be possible through our weekly communal liturgy to worship God in such a way that we also comfort and challenge our people (hopefully without a trace of self-righteousness or triumphalism) in their response to the intimate and arduous poignancy of their daily lives?

I guess not, otherwise we'd do it.

The obscurity of a papal document, the pomposity of an epis-

copal pastoral letter, the aprioristic and empty homily of an inco-
herent parish priest, the cute ideologies of the Prayers over the
People won't cut it because none of these exercises in talking to
ourselves touches the lives of the people whose kids are in our
school or who live down the street or sit in our pews with weary
masks on their faces.

Is it a big order to study these life cycle experiences in the lives
of the laity, to listen to what they say about them, to reflect on
them, and then to try to incorporate creatively into our ministry
and above all our liturgy what we have learned?

I suppose it is. Otherwise we would have done it.

Would it be expensive to launch a survey to find out more
about these intensely human problems into which the Holy Spirit
can and does find room to shower people with grace?

I suppose it would. Otherwise some liturgist, somewhere,
would have suggested it.

So it's a lot easier to worry about where the tabernacle should
be placed or whether to take away holy water during Lent or
when to light the paschal candle or who should receive the Eucharist first, or if scapulars can substitute for chasubles, or
whether there should be music at the end of the Palm Sunday
services. It is still easier to cook up new symbols that somehow the
dullards don't seem to get. It is easiest of all to warn our people
about the temptations of materialism, secularism, and pan-sexual
paganism.

In this book I have argued that the stories, the images, and the
metaphors are the glue that holds Catholic Christianity together
in this time of revolutionary change. The liturgy in all its mani-
festations is an essential component of that glue; it is, to switch
metaphors, the wineskin that did not burst. Yet the arcane de-

bates, the rubrical nit-picking, the authoritarian (and decidedly uncharming) style of many liturgists, and the prolonged and boring performances that they orchestrate have encapsulated the Church's worship in a hard ideological shell.

The Congregation of the Liturgy in Rome has recently argued that the reform of Paul VI is unacceptable because the Enlightenment so heavily influenced it. We are, it would seem, back to the structures (the paradigms and the resources) of the Church immediately after the French Revolution.

Both the Congregation and the ideological liturgists are going after the last remaining wineskin—Catholic imagination.

Conclusion

The Catholic Revolution began on October 13, 1962. Cardinals Lienart and Frings rose to demand a free vote for the members of the commissions that would draft the texts of conciliar documents. With the support of Pope John XXIII, this *event* became the equivalent of the storming of the Bastille. The Council fathers began to realize that they could overcome the entrenched power of the Roman Curia. It would be possible to change the Church, not drastically, it seemed to them, but in certain important areas like liturgy, ecumenism, the interpretation of Scripture, attitudes toward Jews, and religious freedom. With the realization that they had the power to remake the Church, the bishops were swept by a euphoria, an effervescence, an extended moment of collective behavior.

They did not intend to intrude into fundamental doctrine—God, Jesus, Trinity, Eucharist, life after death. They did not intend to make any judgments about such matters as birth control, divorce, or masturbation—to say nothing of the marriage of priests or the ordination of women.[1] They challenged not the authority of the pope but the power of the Roman Curia.

Yet in fact they did destabilize many of the structures of nineteenth-century Catholicism, the paradigms and motivations that oriented Catholicism toward resisting the Enlightenment and Modernity. When they made changes in a Church that most Catholics believed had not changed, would not change, could not change, they swept away the basis of a sin-oriented, blind-obedience relationship between the lay Catholic and the Church leadership.

However, the structures (the old wineskins) proved too weak to permit the infusion of relatively small amounts of change (the new wine). The effervescence the bishops experienced went flat when they returned to the United States. Many of them insisted that nothing had really changed.

In fact, much more had changed than the bishops realized. The effervescence had spread to the lower clergy and almost simultaneously to the laity. Despite what they had been taught, these two groups realized that other changes were possible. The reasons for other resources that supported other structures had never been very persuasive; Catholics had nonetheless supported them because they believed that in the absence of blind obedience to the rules, they would go to hell. Somewhere between 1967 and 1972—probably between 1968 and 1970—the lower clergy and the laity, deeply disturbed by the birth control encyclical, were caught up in their own effervescence and created their own reform. In effect, they pleaded for a freedom of conscience to make their own moral decisions about sex and authority. They would continue to be Catholic, but on their own terms.

Among the structures they destroyed, among the wineskins

they burst were those concerning birth control, divorce, Mass every Sunday, masturbation, and later, in vitro fertilization and homosexuality. Priests and nuns left their vocation by the thousands. The Church seemed to be falling apart.

Did the Council cause the revolution and the resulting chaos and conflict? Actually, the cause was the weakness of the structures, which were unable to absorb even relatively minor changes. The Church had postponed change too long, it had not adjusted its rhetoric and style for the late-twentieth-century well-educated Catholic. The birth control encyclical did not, for example, really try to persuade. Rather, it ordered. It was too late for such demands of blind obedience to work.

In the three decades since the revolution, the conflict has continued between the leadership, which orders, and lower clergy and the laity, which do not in general accept the right of the leadership to give orders on certain issues. Neither side has budged. In fact, the leadership does not even perceive what has happened and is convinced that the problems are consumerism, materialism, secularism, and obsession with sex.

Faith in core religious doctrines has not changed, loyalty to the Catholic heritage has not changed, even the predisposition to choose a spouse who is Catholic has not changed. Nor has the sacramentalism or the communalism of Catholicism, which in fact is what keeps Catholics in the Church.

The emerging new structures of Catholicism involved a loyalty to basic doctrines, including an increase in belief in life after death (Greeley and Hout 1999), a tenacious hold on the imaginative riches of the heritage (the rain forest of metaphors), and the assumption of a right to name one's own conditions for being Catholic. Thus the pope is cheered enthusiastically on various

World Youth Days because he is a powerful metaphor for the Church, but is not heeded when he tries to impose the old rules of sexual ethics.

In the meantime, in the name of the Council, ecumenical and liturgical enthusiasts have set about the stripping of the altars and the devastation of the rain forests, a campaign that, if successful, would deprive the Church of its most powerful, that is to say, its most beautiful and charming, resources.

I do not necessarily approve of all the reforms that the laity and the lower clergy have legislated. Catholics should go to Mass on Sunday whenever they can, simply because they're Catholics and not because they will go to hell if they don't.[2] There is much in the traditional Catholic sexual ethic that deserves careful consideration in the environment of the so-called sexual revolution. I suspect that the sexual ethic will be reconsidered when emphasis shifts from blind obedience to an emphasis on Catholic identity.

This kind of shift, however, will only occur when Church leadership abandons its frantic, if bootless, efforts to restore the status quo ante and begins to listen to what the laity and the lower clergy are trying to say. It must also acknowledge to itself that the Catholic revolution was caused ultimately by the fact that change was delayed too long, with the result that even moderate changes devastated many of the old structures.

Despite the problems that followed the Catholic revolution, the Second Vatican Council was one of the great events in Catholic history. That the excitement, the effervescence, of the years of the Council and the subsequent era has ended in sorrow and bitterness is not the fault of the Council or Pope John. Unfortunately the reform of the Catholic institution, begun so well at the Council, has also ended. Yet the Church must always be reformed if it is to live up to its own vision. The very fact that Catholics participated in the Catholic revolution and redid their view of the Church, in other words, actually strengthened their propensity to stay in the Church, which they view as theirs.

The period of active reform was surely over by 1972. Perhaps it ended with the issuance of the birth control encyclical in 1968. One wonders what would have happened if the leadership of the Church had not lost its nerve and instead had continued the reform to include the Curia and the style of the Papacy itself. The Synod of Bishops was intended to continue the collegiality of the bishops with the pope. However, the Curia, having learned its lesson, has never permitted it to function effectively. If there had been the courage to continue the spirit of conciliar reform, would the effective collapse of communication between the leadership and the lower clergy and the laity have been averted? Would the Church have taken a different direction than the one it has followed for the last three decades? Unfortunately there is no way to answer those questions. Yet could the outcome have been any worse than the present chaos?

Those were exciting times, those days when the Church seemed to be entering a second spring, full of bright promise and dazzling hope. The confidence and hope will return. Those who blighted our hopes, doubtless with the best of intentions, have much for which to answer.

NOTES

INTRODUCTION

1. I have thought out some of the argument of this essay by writing about ideas and insights that have occurred to me through the years. Now that I am preparing to refocus and rearticulate my thoughts up to the present, I have included some of my previous essays, adapting them, sometimes in minor and sometimes in major ways, to the direction of this effort. In the course of my work here I acknowledge my gratitude to the editors of the journals in which these articles originally appeared for permitting me to reuse material from them.

2. I emphasize that this is a book of sociological analysis and not of doctrinal commentary. I must leave to others a theological judgment about the Catholic revolution. Moreover, when I speak of the Catholic imagination I am not rejecting either reason or doctrine. Humans are both reasoning and imagining creatures. A religion without imagination will be sterile (as is most theology today). A religion without rationality can easily become demonic. Catholicism is at the same time powerfully rational and deeply imaginative. Both dimensions are essential. Note that the four most powerful imaginative structures I describe in a later chap-

ter—concern for the poor, Eucharist, Sacraments, and Mary the mother of Jesus—are both crucial doctrines and compelling stories.

1. A CATHOLIC REVOLUTION

1. Most of our research findings in the late 1960s and mid-1970s were rejected out of hand by Catholic priests and bishops—by the former because they were unable to distinguish between opinions and empirical facts and by the latter because the findings were too horrific to contemplate and because they had no need of sociology, the findings of which they could not control.

2. The phrase "on their own terms" infuriates many Church leaders. "You can't name your own terms," they insist. Such an insistence, however, is as useful as admonishing a tsunami to stop its progress. One hopes that the leadership comes to realize that an educated population will lay down its own terms even if it is told that it may not do so. The alternative would be for the term-setting population to leave, which it does not seem inclined to do. One of the great mysteries of the years since the Council is why more Catholics have not left the Church. To many Americans this seems inconsistent and even immoral. "If you disagree with the pope, why don't you leave?" they ask, usually in angry tones. They don't get it that Catholics like being Catholics.

3. I.e., post–World War II.

2. THE "CONFIDENT" CHURCH

1. One may question whether this was ever a serious danger. Neither Protestants who wished to convert Catholics nor bishops trying to prevent such conversion seemed to realize that they never had a chance. Then as now, Catholics liked being Catholics and were not about to give up their religion. Then as now, many do not seem to comprehend this truth.

2. No new parishes or Catholic schools were founded in Chicago between the late 1960s and the late 1990s.

3. To make matters worse, Rome had sent to Chicago an archbishop who was a psychopathic paranoid. He destroyed what little confidence in the Church may have remained.

4. I will address the definition of a "structure" in a subsequent chapter. For the moment, I will describe it as a behavior pattern and the motivational resources that sustain it.

5. Cardinal Stritch of the "confident" Church of Chicago forbade Catholics to attend the first meeting of the World Council of Churches in Evanston, Illinois, in 1947.

6. "Simple," as an adjective modifying laity, usually implies uneducated and illiterate peasants, even when it is used today. The fact that there are few such left in the western world does not seem to matter. The paradigm is too useful as a self-serving justification to yield to fact.

7. It occurred to no one, including the various popes, that as the "prisoner in the Vatican" the pope would come to enjoy unparalleled religious influence and moral prestige among his people.

8. Antonio Rosmini-Serbati was a devout and brilliant Italian priest who was condemned by the Holy Office of the Inquisition in the middle of the nineteenth century and rehabilitated by that organization's successor, the Congregation for the Defense of the Faith, in the early twenty-first. Cardinal Ratzinger, in an exercise in double-think of which only a German theologian would be capable, has defended the consistency of these two processes.

9. De Lubac, Daniélou, and Congar ended up as cardinals, de Lubac and Daniélou having rejected the Vatican Council, Congar only on his deathbed because he had not rejected it.

10. I will not accept an interpretation of this description to mean that I dismiss sin as unimportant. In any orthodox view of Christianity it is very important. However, sin does not exhaust the Catholic heritage.

11. "Does that mean they could not enjoy it?" one of my classmates asked. The Jesuit looked at him with a bemused frown. "Do you think that's possible?"

12. Subsequent research would show that Catholics had become one-fifth of the faculty at top state universities, though they had not

caught up at elite private universities. (It is my impression that they still have not.) Other research revealed that Irish Catholics had caught up with the college attendance rate of the rest of the country in the first decade of the 1900s, and Poles and Italians had caught up in the years after World War II.

13. The education of women would prove to be especially subversive. Education of self or of father did not correlate with dissidence on the part of children in the 1990s but education of mother did.

3. THE WINESKINS BURST

1. Curiously enough, birth control was not an issue in the nineteenth century. It became an issue not so much out of the need to defend Catholic morality from the Enlightenment as out of the need to maintain discipline among the faithful. In the nineteenth century the French Church hierarchy asked the Holy Office several times for a decision on the matter of coitus interruptus. It was told to proceed cautiously and not to disturb the consciences of the laity, a teaching repeated often in conferences for confessors by St. Jean Vianney, the famous curé d'Ars (Noonan 1965). It is a long way from not disturbing the consciences of the laity to George William Mundelein's edict to confessors in the Archdiocese of Chicago in the 1930s. The intervening variable was the decision of the Lambeth Conference in 1930 to legitimate contraception and Pope Pius XI's response condemning it. Contraception went from being a silent issue to becoming a major public issue.

2. Later research would reveal similar change in virtually every Catholic country.

3. As measured by NORC's General Social Survey in 2000 and a 2001 study by Knowledge Network.

4. I must add here that just because I report these dramatic changes, it does not follow that I approve of them. The sociologist describes what has happened and is happening. It is not his task to judge whether the

changes are good or bad. The sociologist may, however, express the opinion that given the context in which the Council occurred, the changes can, in retrospect, be understood. Rules, mortal sin, and the threat of hell were no longer, for weal or woe, enough to prompt lay Catholics to cede control over their sexual lives to Church authority. The call of Archbishop John R. Quinn of San Francisco at the Synod of Bishops in Rome for dialogue between the hierarchy and the laity on the subject does not seem unreasonable. He was, however, promptly slapped down by a member of the Roman Curia.

4. WHAT HAPPENED?

1. Segments of this chapter first appeared in *Commonweal*. I am grateful to the editors for permitting me to reprint them here.

2. Apparently, in this theory, the Holy Spirit cannot be counted on to guide an ecumenical council, but he can be counted on to guide a pope—so long as the pope agrees with us.

3. Cardinal Frings's personal theologian at that time was Joseph Ratzinger, who could be called an important agent of the revolution. In subsequent years, especially as he rose to power in the Church, Ratzinger rejected much of what the Council had achieved—never once acknowledging that he had changed his mind nor explaining theologically how it was possible to repudiate the work of all the bishops of the world as approved by the pope. He changed his mind, without explaining how or why, on liturgical reform, the Synod of Bishops, the power of the national hierarchies, and divorced and remarried Catholics.

4. But only for a time. When the bishops went home, the Curia took over again. It will be a long time before they risk a repetition by permitting all the bishops of the world to gather in Rome. The stage management of the Synod of Bishops (which meets every three years in Rome)—which was supposed to provide for "collegiality" between the pope and his brother bishops—demonstrates that the Curia has learned its lesson.

5. "EFFERVESCENCE" SPREADS FROM THE
COUNCIL TO THE WORLD

1. Wilde 2002. Lecaro was subsequently dismissed from Bologna by Paul VI (despite his support in the Conclave) on a trumped-up charge of financial impropriety.

2. Joseph Ratzinger, as noted before one of the major influences at the Council, has since been eager to take authority away from national conferences of bishops and from the Synod of Bishops. Apparently he distrusts the emotional swings that can occur when bishops assemble. Bishops cannot be trusted when they confuse enthusiasm with the Holy Spirit. Such a position excludes the Holy Spirit from meetings of bishops and calls into question not only Vatican II, but all previous councils of the Church, even if their work has been approved by the pope.

3. As a tourist.

4. The American representative at the Domus Marie was Bishop Ernest Primeau, a native Chicagoan who had become bishop of Manchester, New Hampshire. Wilde's work makes it clear that Primeau was one of the heroes of the Council. Small wonder that the Curia kept him in Manchester until his retirement.

5. Here my analysis goes beyond that of Wilde, but not contrary to her work.

6. Some of those who left the priesthood did so because they were convinced there would be a change and they didn't want to wait. They thought that they would be reintegrated into the priesthood when the change came.

7. Not that the peasants were always blindly obedient.

7. NEW RULES, NEW PROPHETS,
AND BEIGE CATHOLICISM

1. This chapter is based on my personal observations, on various surveys done by the media, and on NORC's annual General Social Survey from 1972 to the present.

2. With, in my judgment, the exception of sensitivity training, which I consider a form of emotional rape.

8. ONLY IN AMERICA?

1. The foreign-language versions of the questionnaire are available from mikehout@uclink4.berkeley.edu.

9. WHY THEY STAY

1. Much of this chapter originally appeared in the magazine *America*. I am grateful to the editors for their permission to reprint.

2. Those who become conservative Protestants apparently find the Catholic Church too lenient; those who become mainline Protestants or reject all religious affiliation apparently find it too strict.

3. James Davidson argues that most sociological studies find an increase in mixed marriages, as though to refute our work by counting the noses of social researchers who agree with him (Davidson et al. 2001). However, most other researchers do not have the data on original religion necessary to determine whether the increase in mixed marriages might be the result of fewer marriage converts.

4. I have tried to argue this thesis at length in my books *Religion as Poetry* and *The Catholic Imagination*. While the reaction to these books has been positive, I'm not sure that many readers understand that I am serious in them: to Catholics, the attraction of Catholicism lies in its stories. Symbols, metaphors, and stories, as I will argue later, are the great resources that remain available to the Church.

5. I have nothing against guitars, but there are other musical instruments of some merit, like the organ, for example.

6. Greeley's Second Law: When the Catholic Church discovers something, everyone else has just abandoned it. And the Third Law: The propensity of a religious institution to tell other institutions how to solve their problems is in inverse proportion to the religious institution's abil-

ity to deal with its own problems. Thus American Catholicism, in a terrible financial crisis (and paying food-stamp wages to many of its own employees), does not hesitate to issue a solemn high pastoral in which it tells the rest of the country of its obligations to the poor and to practice economic justice. The Third Law would seem always to imply a certain amount (usually monumental) of hypocrisy.

7. I am not denying the truths in the catechism, I am merely questioning the pastoral assumptions behind it.

11. RECOVERING THE CATHOLIC HERITAGE

1. Some of this chapter has been published in *Commonweal*. I am grateful to the editors for permission to reprint.

I use the term "heritage" in this chapter instead of "tradition" to bracket some of the theological questions about tradition (as in "scripture and tradition") that I am not competent to discuss. Professor Tilley's luminous book is a major contribution to that subject. It would not, I think, be a mistake to read his book to mean that "tradition" and "heritage" come to practically the same thing.

2. Shea also says that when we invite someone from the past to dinner, we should determine first the subject we want to discuss. In this fantasy, I would invite Pope Gregory the Great to discuss reform of the Papacy. For those who don't think the Papacy needs reform, I invoke the dictum *ecclesia semper reformanda*.

3. Nonetheless, however unintentionally, they have mounted the most serious assault on the sacramental imagination since Bishop Ricci and the Jansenist Synod of Pistoia in the eighteenth century. As Tilley points out, the analogical imagination is one of the five main "grammars" of Catholic tradition (the other four being universal hope, inclusive community, a public church, and a gracious God).

4. A reader of the version of this chapter that appeared in *Commonweal* wrote that she had no need for either the rosary or Gregorian Chant. Patently, I was not suggesting there was such a need for everyone.

Rather, my argument was that they were resources available for those who wanted them.

5. In many recent films—*Always, Ghost, Flatliners,* for example—purgatory or a purgatory-like reality is part of the plot structure. See Bergesen and Greeley 2000.

6. Those, in other words, who paid for the construction of the church. Monsignor Cahalane, my Tucson pastor, keeps the parish church open from early morning to late at night. You can't keep the church open that long, he is told by other priests. It will be open that long, he replies, as long as I'm pastor here.

12. RELIGIOUS EDUCATION AND BEAUTY

1. I proposed something like this style of sacramental administration in my *America* article "Authority as Charm" (parts of which are reprinted in chapter 13 of this book). Several priests wrote to me or to *America* saying that they had tried to be charming at marriages, but it was a waste of time because they never saw the people again. With such an attitude I doubt that they were all that charming. Apparently it never occurred to them that their charm was an investment not just in their parish's future but in the future of the Church.

13. AUTHORITY AS CHARM

1. Much of this chapter originally appeared in *America*. I am grateful for permission to reprint.

2. I am inclined to think that aberrations of the left are not nearly as dangerous to the laity as those of the right. Most lay folk don't understand the dense texts of theologians, but many are easily deceived by more bizarre forms of private revelation.

CONCLUSION

1. Melissa Jo Wilde points out that the reason the Catholic world did not accept *Humanae vitae*, the birth control encyclical, was that the pope did not have the Council behind him. If he had permitted the fathers of the Council to wrestle with that issue, the outcome would perhaps have been different, but the laity and the lower clergy might have been readier to accept whatever decision was made (Wilde 2002).

2. This, I am told, was the intent of the legislation of Lateran Council IV.

REFERENCES

Alberigo, Giuseppe, and Joseph A. Komonchak, eds. 1995–2000. *History of Vatican II.* 3 vols. Maryknoll, NY: Orbis; Leuven: Peeters.

Allen, John L. 2000. *Cardinal Ratzinger: The Vatican's Enforcer of the Faith.* New York: Continuum.

Avella, Steven M. 1992. *This Confident Church: Catholic Leadership and Life in Chicago, 1940–1965.* Notre Dame, IN: University of Notre Dame Press.

Barron, Robert. 2000. "Beyond Beige Catholicism." *Church Magazine,* Summer.

Bergesen, Albert J., and Andrew Greeley. 2000. *God in the Movies: A Sociological Investigation.* New Brunswick, NJ: Transaction Publishers.

Brinton, Crane. 1958. *The Anatomy of Revolution.* New York: Vintage.

Chaves, Mark. 1994. "Secularization as Declining Religious Authority." *Social Forces,* March.

Chaves, Mark, and Peter V. Marsden. 2000. "Congregations and Cultural Capital: Religious Variations in Arts Activity." Paper presented at the annual meeting of the American Sociological Association, Washington, DC, August.

Cornwell, John. 2001. *Breaking Faith: The Pope, the People, and the Fate of Catholicism.* New York: Viking.

Davidson, James D., William d'Antonio, Dean Hoge, and Katherine Meyer. 2001. *American Catholics: Gender, Generation and Commitment.* Walnut Creek, CA: Altamira Press.

Ellis, John Tracy. 1955. *American Catholics and the Intellectual Life. Thought,* Autumn.

Fee, Joan L., Andrew Greeley, William C. McCready, and Teresa A. Sullivan. 1981. *Young Catholics in the United States and Canada.* New York: Sadlier.

Greeley, Andrew. 1994. *Priests Now.* Chicago: NORC.

———. 1995. *Religion as Poetry.* New Brunswick, NJ: Transaction Publishers.

———. 2000. *The Catholic Imagination.* Berkeley: University of California Press.

———. 2003. *Religion in Europe at the End of the Second Millennium: A Sociological Profile.* New Brunswick, NJ: Transaction Publishers.

Greeley, Andrew, and Conor Ward. 2000. "How 'Secularized' Is the Ireland We Live In? Report on a Survey." *Doctrine & Life* (December).

Greeley, Andrew, and Michael Hout. 1999. "Americans' Increasing Belief in Life after Death: Religious Competition or Acculturation." *American Sociological Review* 64, no. 6.

Greeley, Andrew, and Peter H. Rossi. 1966. *The Education of Catholic Americans.* Chicago: Aldine.w

Greeley, Andrew, William McCready, and Kathleen McCourt. 1976. *Catholic Schools in a Declining Church.* Kansas City, MO: Sheed and Ward.

Hoge, Dean R., William D. Dinges, Mary Johnson, and Juan Gonzales, Jr. 2001. *Young Adult Catholics: Religion in the Culture of Choice.* Notre Dame, IN: University of Notre Dame Press.

Hout, Michael, and Andrew Greeley. 1987. "The Center Doesn't Hold:

Church Attendance in the United States, 1940–1984." *American Sociological Review* 52, no. 3 (June).

Johnson, Elizabeth. 2000. "Mary of Nazareth: Friend of God and Prophet." *America* 182, no. 21.

McCallion, Michael J., and David R. Maines. 2000. "Liturgical Problems and the Liturgist." In Helena Z. Lopata and Kevin D. Henson, eds., *Unusual Occupations and Unusually Organized Occupations.* Stamford, CT: JAI Press.

McCarthy, John, and Mayer Zald. 1994. "Resource Mobilizations and Social Movements." *American Journal of Sociology* 82, no. 6.

Noonan, John T. 1965. *Contraception: A History of Its Treatment by the Catholic Theologians and Canonists.* Cambridge, MA: Harvard University Press.

NORC. 1972. *The Catholic Priest in the United States.* Washington, DC: Publications Office, United States Catholic Conference.

O'Dea, Thomas. 1958. *American Catholic Dilemma: An Inquiry into the Intellectual Life.* New York: Sheed and Ward.

O'Malley, John W. 1983. "Developments, Reforms, and Two Great Reformations: Towards a Historical Assessment of Vatican II." *Theological Studies,* no. 44.

———. 2002. "The Scandal: A Historian's Perspective." *America* 186, no. 18.

Sewell, William, Jr. 1992. "A Theory of Structure: Duality, Agency, and Transformation." *American Journal of Sociology* 98, no. 1 (July).

———. 1996. "Three Temporalities: Toward an 'Eventful' Sociology." In Terrence J. McDonald, ed., *The Historic Turn in the Human Sciences.* Ann Arbor: University of Michigan Press.

Tilley, Terrence. 2000. *Inventing Catholic Tradition.* Maryknoll, NY: Orbis.

Tracy, David. 1981. *The Analogical Imagination.* New York: Crossroad.

Weigel, Gustave. 1957. "American Catholic Intellectualism: A Theologian's Reflections." *Review of Politics,* July.

Wilde, Melissa Jo. 2002. "Reconstructing Religion: A Sociological

Study of Vatican Council II." Ph.D. diss., University of California, Berkeley.

Wills, Garry. 2000. *Papal Sin: Structures of Deceit*. New York: Doubleday.

Zald, Mayer, and Michael Berger. 1978. "Social Movements in Organizations." *American Journal of Sociology* 83, no. 4.

INDEX

Compositor: Binghamton Valley Composition, LLC
Text: 10/15 Janson
Display: Janson
Printer and binder: Maple-Vail Manufacturing Group